List of resources on the CD-ROM

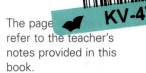

The page
refer to the teacher's
notes provided in this
book.

INTRODUCTION

This book and CD-ROM support the teaching and learning set out in the QCA Scheme of Work for history in Years 3 and 4. The CD provides a large bank of varied visual and aural resources. The book provides teacher's notes, background information, ideas for discussion and activities to accompany the CD resources, along with photocopiable pages to support teaching and learning. All have been specially chosen to meet the requirements outlined in the QCA units on the Second World War, Ancient Egypt and Local history. Additional resources and ideas have also been included to enable teachers to broaden these areas of study if they wish, such as interviews and statistics. The resources are also relevant and useful to those not necessarily following the QCA Schemes of Work, particularly teachers in Scotland.

The resources and activities are not intended to be used rigidly, however, since they do not provide a structure for teaching in themselves. The teacher's notes provide ideas for discussion and activities that focus on the 'Knowledge, skills and understanding' of the National Curriculum for history. They aim to guide teachers in developing the skills and concepts that are fundamental to children's understanding of what it is to learn about the past.

In this book, there is an emphasis on developing children's awareness and understanding of chronology, of asking and answering questions, and of investigating historical sources and communicating findings in a variety of ways. Above all, the activities and discussions aim to build clear links between the firsthand experience they gain from using the resources on the CD and their developing awareness of the past.

Links with other subjects
Research skills
Independent enquiry and the development of research skills are important in this book. Often, the activities are based on children's use of reference books, fiction and non-fiction sources and the Internet to gather further information related to a topic or individual. Work of this kind will help foster an independent, enquiring attitude on the part of the children, helping them to become more effective learners, genuinely interested in broadening their knowledge of people and events. Through examining the images provided on the CD, children will naturally become involved in the technique of raising questions and then working to find the answers.

Literacy
There are a number of close links with the topics covered in this book and work on literacy. The discussion activities contribute directly to the requirements for speaking and listening, as do the drama and role-play activities. Both discussion points and suggested activities contribute to the requirements of the National Curriculum for reading and writing, and relate to Literacy Hour activities. The stories and accounts may be used in shared reading during the Literacy Hour, or to provide a stimulus for shared, guided or independent writing. Similarly, the writing frames may be used to support guided or independent writing. Images from the CD could be used to stimulate independent reading, writing and research, or to illustrate it. They may also be used to illustrate the timelines created in the course of each topic.

Art and design
There are close links with art and creativity. Much work at Key Stage 2 needs to be visual. Wherever possible, therefore, the activities in this book are based on visual sources and extensive use of drawing to extend the children's understanding of a particular topic or concept. For example, in drawing pictures of wartime bombing raids they will develop their observational skills and improve accuracy in their artwork. Working with photographs of people, sculptures and various archaeological sources will also develop their skills in source analysis through the use of art in its many different forms.

ICT
Finally, there are clear links with information technology. These skills are constantly in use in the activities in the book, for example when children record the results of their own research. The Internet is particularly useful in terms of providing an inexhaustible resource for children to use in carrying out their own research into specific aspects of each topic.

 # Contents

Exmouth

**IF YOU ACCEPT THE ABOVE CONDITIONS YOU MAY PROCEED
TO USE THIS CD-ROM**

Text © Pat Hoodless
© 2003 Scholastic Ltd

Published by Scholastic Ltd, Villiers House,
Clarendon Avenue, Leamington Spa,
Warwickshire CV32 5PR

Printed by Bell & Bain Ltd, Glasgow

3 4 5 6 7 8 9 0   5 6 7 8 9 0 1 2

British Library Cataloguing-in-Publication Data
A catalogue record for this book is available from
the British Library.

ISBN 0-439-98452-1

Visit our website at
www.scholastic.co.uk

CD developed in association with
Footmark Media Ltd

Author
Pat Hoodless

Editor
Christine Harvey

Assistant Editor
Dulcie Booth

Series Designer
Joy Monkhouse

Designer
Catherine Mason

Cover photographs
© Photodisc,
© Popperfoto,
© Werner Forman Archive,
© AKG, London

Acknowledgements

The publisher wishes to thank **The British Museum** for the use of an extract from *The Scribe* from the website www.ancientegypt.co.uk © 2003, The British Museum; **Anne Serraillier** for an extract from *The Silver Sword* by Ian Serraillier © 1956, Ian Serraillier (1956, Jonathan Cape); **Megan Saxelby** for her involvement with the interview.

Extracts from the National Curriculum for England © Crown copyright material is reproduced with the permission of the Controller of HMSO and the Queen's Printer for Scotland.

Every effort has been made to trace copyright holders and the publishers apologise for any omissions.

HOW TO USE THE CD-ROM

Windows NT users
If you use Windows NT you may see the following error message: 'The procedure entry point Process32First could not be located in the dynamic link library KERNEL32.dll'. Click on **OK** and the CD will autorun with no further problems.

Setting up your computer for optimal use
On opening, the CD will alert you if changes are needed in order to operate the CD at its optimal use. There are three changes you may be advised to make:

Viewing resources at their maximum screen size
To see images at their maximum screen size, your screen display needs to be set to 800 x 600 pixels. In order to adjust your screen size you will need to **Quit** the program.

If using a PC, open the **Control Panel**. Select **Display** and then **Settings**. Adjust the **Desktop Area** to 800 x 600 pixels. Click on **OK** and then restart the program.

If using a Mac, from the **Apple** menu select **Control Panels** and then **Monitors** to adjust the screen size.

Adobe Acrobat Reader
To print high-quality versions of images and to view and print the photocopiable pages on the CD you need **Adobe Acrobat Reader** installed on your computer. If you do not have it installed already, a version is provided on the CD. To install this version **Quit** the 'Ready Resources' program.

If using a PC, right-click on the **Start** menu on your desktop and choose **Explore**. Click on the **+** sign to the left of the CD drive entitled 'Ready Resources' and open the folder called 'Acrobat Reader Installer'. Run the program contained in this folder to install **Adobe Acrobat Reader**.

If using a Mac, double click on the 'Ready Resources' icon on the desktop and on the 'Acrobat Reader Installer' folder. Run the program contained in this folder to install **Adobe Acrobat Reader**.

PLEASE NOTE: If you do not have **Adobe Acrobat Reader** installed, you will not be able to print high-quality versions of images, or to view or print photocopiable pages (although these are provided in the accompanying book and can be photocopied).

QuickTime
In order to view the videos and listen to the audio on this CD you will need to have **QuickTime version 5 or later** installed on your computer. If you do not have it installed already, or have an older version of **QuickTime**, the latest version is provided on the CD. If you choose to install this version, **Quit** the 'Ready Resources' program.

If using a PC, right-click on the **Start** menu on your desktop and choose **Explore**. Click on the **+** sign to the left of the CD drive that is entitled 'Ready Resources' and open the folder called 'QuickTime Installer'. Run the program contained in this folder to install **QuickTime**.

If using a Mac, double click on the 'Ready Resources' CD icon on the desktop and then on the 'Acrobat Reader Installer' folder. Run the program contained in this folder to install **QuickTime**.

PLEASE NOTE: If you do not have **QuickTime** installed you will be unable to view the films.

Menu screen
▶ Click on the **Resource Gallery** of your choice to view the resources available under that topic.
▶ Click on **Complete Resource Gallery** to view all the resources available on the CD.
▶ Click on **Photocopiable Resources (PDF format)** to view a list of the photocopiables provided in the book that accompanies this CD.
▶ **Back**: click to return to the **opening screen**. Click **Continue** to move to the **Menu screen**.
▶ **Quit**: click **Quit** to close the menu program and progress to the **Quit screen.** If you quit from the **Quit screen** you will exit the CD. If you do not quit you will return to the **Menu screen**.

Resource Galleries
▶ **Help**: click **Help** to find support on accessing and using images.
▶ **Back to menu:** click here to return to the **Menu screen**.
▶ **Quit:** click here to move to the **Quit screen** – see **Quit** above.

Viewing images

Small versions of each image are shown in the Resource Gallery. Click and drag the slider on the slide bar to scroll through the images in the Resource Gallery, or click on the arrows to move the images frame by frame. Roll the pointer over an image to see the caption.

▶ Click on an image to view the screen-sized version of it.

▶ To return to the Resource Gallery click on **Back to Resource Gallery**.

Viewing videos

Click on the video icon of your choice in the Resource Gallery. In order to view the videos on this CD, you will need to have **QuickTime** installed on your computer (see 'Setting up your computer for optimal use' above).

Once at the video screen, use the buttons on the bottom of the video screen to operate the video. The slide bar can be used for a fast forward and rewind. To return to the Resource Gallery click on **Back to Resource Gallery**.

Listening to sound recordings

Click on the required sound icon. Use the buttons or the slide bar to hear the sound. A transcript will be displayed on the viewing screen where appropriate. To return to the Resource Gallery, click on **Back to Resource Gallery**.

Printing

Click on the image to view it (see 'Viewing images' above). There are two print options:

Print using Acrobat enables you to print a high-quality version of an image. Choosing this option means that the image will open as a read-only page in **Adobe Acrobat** and in order to access these files you will need to have already installed **Adobe Acrobat Reader** on your computer (see 'Setting up your computer for optimal use' above). To print the selected resource, select **File** and then **Print**. Once you have printed the resource **minimise** or **close** the Adobe screen using — or **X** in the top right-hand corner of the screen. Return to the Resource Gallery by clicking on **Back to Resource Gallery**.

Simple print enables you to print a lower quality version of the image without the need to use **Adobe Acrobat Reader**. Select the image and click on the **Simple print** option. After printing, click on **Back to Resource Gallery**.

Slideshow presentation

If you would like to present a number of resources without having to return to the Resource Gallery and select a new image each time, you can compile a slideshow. Click on the **+** tabs at the top of each image in the Resource Gallery you would like to include in your presentation (pictures, sound and video can be included). It is important that you click on the images in the order in which you would like to view them (a number will appear on each tab to confirm the order). If you would like to change the order, click on **Clear slideshow** and begin again. Once you have selected your images – up to a maximum of 20 – click on **Play slideshow** and you will be presented with the first of your selected resources. To move to the next selection in your slideshow click on **Next slide**, to see a previous resource click on **Previous slide**. You can end your slideshow presentation at any time by clicking on **Resource Gallery**. Your slideshow selection will remain selected until you **Clear slideshow** or return to the **Menu screen**.

Viewing on an interactive whiteboard or data projector

Resources can be viewed directly from the CD. To make viewing easier for a whole class, use a large monitor, data projector or interactive whiteboard. For group, paired or individual work, the resources can be viewed from the computer screen.

Photocopiable resources (PDF format)

To view or print a photocopiable resource page, click on the required title in the list and the page will open as a read-only page in **Adobe Acrobat**. In order to access these files you will need to have already installed **Adobe Acrobat Reader** on your computer (see 'Setting up your computer for optimal use' above). To print the selected resource select **File** and then **Print**. Once you have printed the resource **minimise** or **close** the Adobe screen using — or **X** in the top right-hand corner of the screen. This will take you back to the list of PDF files. To return to the **Menu screen**, click on **Back**.

SECOND WORLD WAR

Content, skills and concepts

This chapter on the Second World War relates to Unit 9 of the QCA Scheme of Work for history at Key Stage 2, 'What was it like for children in the Second World War?'. It is assumed that this unit will be taught mainly to Years 3 or 4, but it could also be adapted for teaching children in older year groups.

Children will already have gained experience while working on other history units by this stage. Recounting stories about the past, and looking for similarities and differences between the past and the present, are prior learning activities that will have introduced relevant skills and concepts to the children before they progress to the skills and concepts required in this unit. The chapter includes suggestions for the extension of these and other skills, such as recognising cause and effect. It also introduces to children knowledge and understanding of a major event in world history.

Resources on the CD-ROM

The Second World War Resource Gallery on the CD offers a range of resources, such as photographs, posters, factual information and stories. An archive film showing the destruction of Manchester during the Blitz is included as well as an interview with a survivor of the Coventry Blitz. This chapter suggests how all the resources can be used in teaching about the effects of the Second World War, with a particular focus on the experiences of children.

Photocopiable pages

Photocopiable resources can be found at the end of this chapter and are also provided in PDF format on the CD-ROM, from which they can be printed. They include:
▶ a timeline
▶ word cards which highlight the essential vocabulary of this topic
▶ texts, ranging from blackout rules to a story about life during wartime.
The teacher's notes to accompany these resources include suggestions for developing discussion about them and ways of using them for whole class, group or individual activities.

Texts

The factual rules associated with blackouts and rationing bring a note of reality to the topic. The story attempts to develop this understanding of the reality of war further, to include the experience of children during wartime. These texts have been written at different reading levels to enable teachers to use them for shared reading or to share with a group, as part of a guided reading session. More able readers may be able to read the texts independently.

History skills

Skills such as observing, describing, using time-related vocabulary, sequencing, using a timeline, understanding the meaning of dates, comparing, inferring, listening, speaking, reading, writing and drawing are involved in the activities. For example, there is an opportunity for children to develop independent skills in sequencing through the use of the timeline, which outlines the key events of the war, and for them to learn to use descriptive vocabulary to describe the maps, posters and photographs included on the CD.

Historical understanding

A further overarching aim in the activities is for children to begin to develop a more detailed knowledge of the past and an ability to sequence events independently, through understanding of the context and content of factual information. They will begin to give reasons for events, use sources to find further information and be able to recount and rewrite the stories and accounts they have heard, using different forms of presentation. They will also have the opportunity to extend their skills in using descriptive language and specific time-related terms by beginning to write their own factual accounts of the past.

NOTES ON THE CD-ROM RESOURCES

Second World War map

This map shows the world in 1940, when countries had joined either the Allies or the Axis powers. The white areas of the map show the Allies – Britain and the Commonwealth and the countries that supported them. The black areas indicate the Axis powers, led by Germany and Italy, and those countries they were occupying. The lighter-striped areas represent the countries that decided to remain neutral, not supporting either side. The darker-striped areas show the French colonial territories. Some of these countries supported Free France, under the leadership of General de Gaulle, and others supported the Vichy regime of Marshall Pétain, which meant that they effectively came under German control. However, in 1942, when the British army defeated the Germans and Italians in North Africa, all these West African countries became supporters of Free France. The main feature of the map is the way it shows how the entire world was affected by the alliances made during the war.

Discussing the map

▶ Before looking at the map, ask the children to talk about what they already know about the Second World War.

▶ Study the map carefully with them, ensuring that they recognise the continents, and where Britain and Europe are located.

▶ Talk about the meaning of the words in the map's key, such as *Allies, Axis, Neutral, colonial territories*.

▶ Ask for volunteers to read the key and to link the information in the key to the shading on the map.

▶ Focus on the areas which supported the Allies and discuss why they are distributed around the world. Ask the children to think about the reason for this (the Commonwealth countries were included in this group). Then consider the distribution of the Axis powers around the world.

▶ Ask the children to suggest why some countries wanted to be neutral.

▶ Refer the children back to the map as a whole and ask them, now that they have considered it, to explain why the war was called a *World War*.

Activities

▶ Give each of the children a copy of the map and ask them to label the continents and leading countries involved in the war, such as Britain, Germany, France, Russia, the USA, Italy, Japan, Australia.

▶ Create a series of map overlays, showing German expansion into Austria, Poland, Belgium and France. Use these overlays on an OHP to show the build-up culminating in the position shown on the 'Second World War map' and discuss the reasons for Hitler's desire to take over other parts of the world (to unite the German-speaking peoples, to acquire an Empire, to gain access to sea ports).

▶ Help the children to write about some of the reasons for the alliances that were made with Britain, for example historical connections, the Commonwealth, a common desire to resist the spread of Fascism.

▶ Use the timeline on photocopiable page 27 to reinforce in the children's minds the period in which the war took place. They may be able to remember some key dates.

Sir Winston Churchill

Sir Winston Churchill was famous during the Second World War for the sign he can be seen making in this photograph, which he called the 'V for Victory' sign. It is now often known by people as a sign meaning 'peace'. Churchill took over the leadership of the coalition government in Britain soon after the start of the war. He had been warning for some time before the war that a policy of appeasement would not succeed with Hitler, and he ultimately proved to be a very suitable person to lead the British war effort. He was a powerful speaker, able to instil courage and pride in his audiences. Many of his speeches became famous, particularly the 'Fight them on the beaches' speech. He worked tirelessly, sometimes working in a small underground office in London to avoid the disruption of the air raids.

Discussing the photograph

▶ Ask the children if they have ever seen this person before, and explain, if necessary, who he was.

▶ Talk about his position as Prime Minister during the war, and explain what a coalition government is.

▶ Ask the children to look at Churchill's appearance. Discuss why he might have had his photograph taken in ordinary, or civilian clothes (to look more appealing to the people).

▶ Look at the sign he is making and ask if anyone can explain what it symbolised.

▶ Tell the children about Churchill's speeches and the effect he had on the people of Britain during the war. Ask the children why they think this was important.

▶ Can the children suggest what features of Churchill's appearance may have given people confidence in him?

Activities

▶ Ask the children to suggest a collection of adjectives to describe Churchill in the photograph. Add these to the class word bank.

▶ Ask the children to research in books, CD-ROMs and using the Internet, things that Churchill did during the war. Ask them to write a report about two things they find out.

▶ Give the children a matrix for them to draw the features in the photograph that look old-fashioned.

▶ Get the children to study the photograph very closely and to give brief verbal descriptions of what they think Churchill was like as a person, such as *He appears serious, but also seems quite jolly*; *He looks very tired, but tries to look defiant with his 'Victory' sign.*

Adolf Hitler

This photograph shows Adolf Hitler, the German Führer, who led Germany both into fascism and the Second World War. Here, he is leading the German army in its march into the Sudetenland in Czechoslovakia, at the border at Wildenau, in October 1938. It was Hitler's decision to go on to invade Poland, after already having annexed Austria and Czechoslovakia, that finally triggered the declaration of war by Britain. Britain had announced that she would fight if Hitler went ahead and invaded Poland, which he did on 1 September 1939. Hitler was infamous for his plan to rid Germany and Europe of all Jews, whom he blamed for the troubles of the German people in the 1930s. He was a small man in stature, known for his characteristic moustache and for the Nazi salute which he always used. This photograph shows him driving past rows of German troops, some of whom are saluting him with the Nazi salute. Hitler appears composed, confident and is extremely smart in his military uniform. He is thought to have committed suicide in a bunker in Berlin just before Germany finally surrendered at the end of the war in Europe in 1945, but his body has never been found.

Discussing the photograph

▶ Ask the children to look carefully at the picture and ask if they have seen the man in the car before. Explain who Hitler was, and his position, if necessary.

▶ Ask the children who the people are that are watching him go by. Some seem to be walking along with the car. Discuss why this is (they are probably his bodyguards).

▶ Draw the children's attention to the salutes that some of the soldiers are making. Explain how this was a special salute of the Nazis who supported Hitler.

▶ Ask if the children can see a special symbol that the Nazis wore, and had on their flags (a Nazi at the front-right of the photograph has a swastika on his armband). Explain that the symbol was called a swastika.

▶ Talk about the features of Hitler's appearance that characterise him, such as his moustache, his uniform.

▶ Explain to the children that the photograph shows Hitler leading the invasion into Czechoslovakia in 1938. Show them where this is on a map of Europe (now the Czech Republic and Slovakia).

Activities
▶ Review the timeline on photocopiable page 27 with the children and note also how Hitler had gained power in Germany long before the war. Ask them to extend the timeline and mark key dates, such as 1933, when he became Chancellor, and 1934, when he became leader, or Fuhrer, in Germany.

▶ Ask the children to imagine they are newspaper reporters, watching the event in the photograph. Tell them to write a report explaining the event to send back to their newspaper for the next day.

▶ Provide books and other materials for the children to find out about the Hitler Youth Movement, which many young people joined when Hitler was in power.

A British aeroplane

This is a photograph of a Lancaster bomber, a type of aeroplane that was widely used during the Second World War. It has a large cockpit and an additional area for the crew near the back of the aeroplane. Men were able to operate guns from these points to protect the aeroplane from enemy attack from any direction. The aeroplanes were quite large, and needed four propeller engines to carry the heavy load of bombs, which were released as they flew over enemy targets. The British aeroplanes could be recognised from the RAF circular symbol painted on the wings and body of the aircraft.

A German aeroplane

This is a photograph of a Dornier aeroplane, of the type used by Germany in the bombing of Britain. It has a large cockpit at the front, giving a very wide view of any approaching aircraft. Smaller than the Lancaster, the Dornier has two propeller engines. It bears the symbol of the German airforce, the Luftwaffe, in the shape of a double cross, on its sides and wings. In 1940 the Battle of Britain took place between the RAF and the Luftwaffe, as the German planes tried to gain dominance in British skies.

Discussing the photographs
▶ Before looking at the photographs, talk to the children about how Hitler began to invade many countries in Europe and explain that it was when he invaded Poland that Britain and France declared war on Germany.

▶ Discuss how the war was fought, explaining how each side tried to weaken the other by carrying out mass bombing raids on each other's major cities and towns. Tell the children how planes like these would fly over a town and drop many bombs all at once, causing a lot of damage. Explain how they usually flew at night because they were less likely to get shot down by the defending anti-aircraft guns, which were called 'ack-ack' guns because of the sound they made.

▶ Look at the photograph of 'A British aeroplane' and ask the children what type of plane they think it shows. Discuss whether it was a large or small plane. Show them 'A German aeroplane' and ask them which plane looks the biggest.

▶ Point out the number of engines each plane had and the special area at the back, where gunners would sit in the British plane.

▶ Ask how the children can tell which plane is British, and which plane is German.

Activities
▶ Get the children to compare the two photographs and to note the similarities and differences between the two planes, recording their findings on a grid.

▶ Use the word cards on photocopiable page 24 to reinforce the children's understanding of words such as *air raid* and *bomb damage*.

▶ Challenge the children to ask other adults at home about wartime aeroplanes, and suggest they make a list of those they can find out about. They can then carry out further personal research into two or three selected examples.

▶ Provide a wide variety of art materials for the children to create their own scenes of war planes, either in battle in the sky or dropping bombs over streets of houses or factories.

▶ Provide the children with strips of paper to divide into boxes and make into strip cartoons. Using these they can draw a sequence of pictures and write short captions about a wartime airman's adventure.

▶ Play 'Video: Manchester took it too' (provided on the CD) to show the children bomb damage caused by aeroplanes.

Blitz damage

The Luftwaffe began bombing London in September 1940 in what became known as the Blitz (from the German *blitzkrieg* which meant *lightning war*).

This photograph shows a double-decker bus after it has been wrecked by a bombing raid in Holborn, London, in 1940. The bomb appears to have hit the building immediately behind the bus, damaging other buildings nearby. Only the skeleton of the building next to the bus remains standing. The bus itself has been almost flattened by the blast from the bomb, which hit the opposite side from that seen in the picture. A few men can be seen walking through the wreckage of the building, probably assessing damage. The people travelling on the bus were probably killed.

Discussing the photograph

[Sensitivity will be needed when discussing this photograph since some children may find scenes like this disturbing. Take particular care if refugee children are included in the class.]

▶ Allow plenty of time for the children to take in what has happened in this photograph before discussing what has happened to the buildings and the street, and how it happened.

▶ Can the children identify the bus?

▶ Ask the children where they think the bomb landed.

▶ Discuss what has happened to the building next to where the bomb landed and what has happened to the bus.

▶ Discuss what it must have been like for the people caught up in the bomb blast, and get the children to think about the effect on everyday life of the Blitz. Discuss, in particular, how children might have been affected.

▶ Talk about the effects of war on modern-day children today in countries like Afghanistan, Israel and Palestine.

Activities

See 'Moving house in the Blitz', below.

Moving house in the Blitz

This family have had to collect any belongings they can find from their house which has been destroyed by German bombing. Taken in October 1940, the photograph shows how hard it must have been for families like this. They had to find whatever means of transport they could and then find a new home. What is amazing is the courage and confidence they seem to show on their faces. The mother has rescued her pot plant and has a brave smile on her face. During the war, this spirit of defiance was reinforced by a strong sense of community, where neighbours and friends, as well as family, supported each other as much as they could.

Discussing the photograph

▶ Ask the children what they think has happened in this photograph.

▶ Discuss who the people might be, for example they might be the family from the house in the background which has been destroyed.

▶ Look at the detail in the picture and ask for volunteers to find some of the things they are taking away from what was their home. Can anyone suggest why they are taking things like the pot plant?

▶ Discuss how difficult it must have been to move things, as transport was limited and difficult to get hold of during the Blitz.

▶ Ask them to think about the feelings of the young boy in shorts in the picture. Focus the children on his expression and ask them to guess what he may have been thinking.

Activities

▶ Use the word cards on photocopiable page 24 to familiarise the children with key words such as *the Blitz* and *bomb damage*.

▶ Remind, or explain to, the children that the Blitz took place early in the war, and was at its worst during 1940. Get them to find this on the timeline on photocopiable page 27.

▶ Suggest the children work in pairs to create some free verse to express how they might have felt, or how the young boy in the 'Moving house in the Blitz' photograph might have felt, during the Blitz.

▶ Get the children to devise a list of interview questions that they would like to ask a child who was alive during the Blitz, for example *What was done to try to prevent the bombs landing on the city?*

▶ Play the class 'Interview: Experiencing the Blitz' (provided on the CD) and ask the children to compare the experiences that Mrs Saxelby experienced with what the two photographs show.

Children in the ruins

Here we can see a group of children clambering among the ruined remains of a bombed building. From the building's large windows and the iron frames, of what may have been desks, visible in the rubble, it could be concluded that this was once a school. This may also help to explain why there are so many children, who appear to be searching among the debris. They may be looking for lost belongings of theirs, such as books. They certainly look very intent on finding anything of use.

The photograph shows the material loss of their school and classroom, but also symbolises the personal loss that children suffered at this time, of their own belongings and possibly of their learning and schooling. It shows how deeply devastating bombing of a civilian population was on several different levels.

Discussing the photograph

▶ Look carefully at the photograph with the class, and ask the children what is particularly striking about it (that there are only children shown).

▶ Discuss what the children in the photograph appear to be doing.

▶ Look at the building and ask the children to think what sort of building it could have been, giving reasons for their suggestions. Suggest, if necessary, that it may have been a school.

▶ Discuss what the children may have been searching for.

▶ Consider the significance of all the things the children may have lost. This could include things such as their school and their opportunity to learn, their books and work, their personal belongings.

▶ Get the children to think about the effects on the children of losing so much so suddenly. Talk about how they themselves might feel if this happened to them. What things might they miss if their school was bombed during the night?

Activities

▶ Review the timeline (photocopiable page 27) with the children and note the date of the Blitz.

▶ Look at a map of Britain and discuss the areas likely to have been heavily bombed during the Blitz. Ask the children, in groups, to discuss and write about why they think these areas were targeted (where there were munitions factories, such as in Birmingham and Coventry; ports).

▶ Challenge the children to write a letter to a friend, telling them about how their school has been destroyed and what they have lost. This could be set in the past, during the Blitz, or in the present.

Sandbags

In this photograph we can see a man making a call in a telephone box during the Second World War. The photograph was taken in London's West End in September 1939, very shortly after the outbreak of the war. The picture looks quite strange and amusing today, with the box almost completely covered with sandbags. These were used to protect the telephone box from bomb blasts and to help sound proof it against the noise of air raid sirens, aircraft and exploding bombs.

Sandbags were a common feature of wartime life for people in Britain. They were used everywhere to try and protect buildings or facilities. They were used to protect facilities such as fire stations and other important buildings, such as town halls or cathedrals. They were also used in a domestic context, to protect air-raid shelters in people's gardens.

Sheltering in the Underground

Families in many parts of Britain would have used their own small air-raid shelters in their back gardens to protect themselves from air raids when they were at home. However, air raids were almost constant during the Blitz which began in September 1940 in London, and people were often caught away from home and needed somewhere safe to go during an air raid, or simply felt safer in the deep underground stations. Londoners set up their own sleeping equipment in the 80 tube stations that were used to begin with, but the beds in this photograph look as though they have been erected for permanent use.

Discussing the photographs

▶ Look at both photographs and ask the children why they think the people are living in this way. Discuss where it is that the people are sleeping in the 'Sheltering in the Underground' photograph, and explain about the London Underground if necessary.

▶ Discuss how, soon after the start of the war, it became apparent that bombs were going to be used against civilians rather than gas which had initially been feared (see also 'Gas poster', page 16). Gas masks were still kept available, however, as a precaution.

▶ Look at the 'Sandbags' photograph. Can the children tell you what is in the sacks that have been stacked around the telephone box?

▶ Ask the children what the effect of putting the sandbags around the telephone box would be (to protect it from the blast of explosions).

▶ Look at the photograph 'Sheltering in the Underground' and discuss what arrangements have been made for people to sleep there. Note how some are sleeping on the floor and everyone is squashed together. Ask the children what they think it must have been like to shelter in the Underground. (Move them towards thinking about what it must have been like to have little sleep for weeks and weeks and discuss how dirty and dusty it must have been.)

▶ Ask the children what they notice about the people and the things in the photographs. Ask if telephone boxes look like the one in the photograph today. Do people dress like the people in these photographs today?

Activities

▶ Help the children to locate the date of the Blitz on the timeline on photocopiable page 27.

▶ Work with the class to produce a list of adjectives which describe conditions in London and other cities during the Blitz. Set the children the task of writing some short verses about sleeping in the Underground, using some of the adjectives from the list collected.

▶ Ask the children to refer to books and to use the Internet to find out about other kinds of shelters used in Britain during the Blitz, such as Anderson shelters.

▶ Let each child make a class book about life in Britain during the Second World War. Work based on the photocopiable pages 28–9 could also be kept in these.

▶ Tell the children about the bombs commonly known at the time as 'doodle bugs'. These were Hitler's 'flying bombs'. They were remote controlled and their engines stopped just before they came down and exploded. People used to listen for the engines cutting out. Ask the children to imagine the sounds of bombs landing and explosions, and to make a collection of adjectives and verbs to describe these.

▶ Ask if they can see any children in the photographs. Discuss what had happened to the children from major cities by this point in the war. Use the photograph 'Evacuees' (provided on the CD) to help explain.

Air raid siren

This is a sound recording of an air raid siren used in the Second World War. The siren would start to sound as soon as enemy aircraft were spotted, to warn the civilian population to take shelter before the bombing began. Survivors of the war who experienced these sounds say that the sound of the sirens made them feel very shaky and apprehensive, and that this sound still has the same effect on them today, conjuring up feelings of dread and horror. Many say that it was one of the worst memories they have of the war.

Discussing the sound

▶ Play the recording and ask the children if they have ever heard this sound before. If not, ask if they can guess what it was.

▶ Tell the children that the siren was often heard during the Second World War, and explain what it was used for.

▶ Discuss how some people today might hear a similar sound, since some factories use it to let workers know that it is time to start or stop work.

▶ Ask the children what they think the effect of the sound would have been on people. What did it make the children feel like when they first heard it? Tell them how it was a really terrifying noise for people to hear in the war, and discuss the reasons for this.

▶ Talk about how people in other countries that were bombed during the war, such as Germany and France, would have felt the same. Show the children the photograph 'Dresden after the bombing' (provided on the CD) to reinforce the German people's similar experiences with the children.

Activities

▶ Provide the children with a selection of musical instruments and let them experiment with making 'siren' noises.

▶ Use these sound effects as the backdrop for a short drama about an air raid, which the children can develop and act out.

▶ Explain how even today, survivors of the war who hear the siren sound still feel horrified. Play the children the interview 'Experiencing the Blitz' and focus on the part where Mrs Saxelby talks about how hearing the siren today makes her feel.

Video: Manchester took it too

This video clip shows the devastation caused in Manchester when it was heavily bombed in December, 1940. It is a useful piece of film footage in that it shows how many other parts of the country, as well as London, were badly damaged during the Blitz. The video clip shows scenes of smoke rising and buildings collapsing, accompanied by the sounds of explosions. The intensity and extent of the damage is quite shocking and far greater than anyone would imagine possible today. The flames and smoke are bravely tackled by the firemen, who struggle with their long hose pipes to reach the tall buildings that have been damaged.

The commentary is a very interesting feature of the video clip in the way it emphasises not just the damage and horror of the experience, but also the courage of the Manchester people and of their firemen. The narrator points out how the bombing will always be remembered and uses many metaphorical allusions to convey the conflicting feelings of outrage and pride experienced by people during these times.

Discussing the video

▶ Play the video clip two or three times. It is a short extract, but it contains a great deal of information for the children to absorb. Several viewings may, therefore, be needed for them to take in everything.

▶ Ask the children to notice the writing on the video and also to listen carefully to the commentary. They may need to see it a few times in order to focus their attention on the commentary.

▶ Discuss the name of the video, 'Manchester took it too'. Ask the children why they think it is called this. Explain how most interest was focused on London during the Blitz and the film makers were trying to show how towns in the north of the country suffered in the same way.

▶ Discuss what kind of damage is shown in the video and ask the children how they felt when they saw this. Ask if the damage is greater than they thought it probably was.

▶ Talk about what is left of many buildings. Discuss the danger associated with these ruins.

▶ Ask the children what they think happened to life and business in towns when this sort of damage had taken place.

▶ Ask the children to recall the comments made by the narrator on the film. Discuss what he says about the damage.

▶ Ask them what else the narrator says, for example about the people and the firemen.

▶ Point out the metaphorical phrases he uses, such as *flames of war*, *heart of Manchester*, *heart of the north*, and ask the class to explain what each of these phrases mean. Discuss why he uses such words and phrases.

▶ Talk about the children's impression of the commentary and of the people's reaction in Manchester to the bombing.

▶ Tell the class how the bombing damaged many important buildings in Manchester, such as the cathedral, the station at Piccadilly, the market and the Free Trade Hall.
▶ Talk about how many of the old buildings were unsafe after the bombing and had to be pulled down. Explain how much of Manchester has now been rebuilt.

Activities
▶ Help the children to locate the date of the Blitz on the timeline (photocopiable page 27).
▶ Ask them to locate Manchester on a map of Britain.
▶ Organise the children into small groups to watch the video clip with no sound and ask them to write brief commentaries in their own words.
▶ Still working in groups, set the children the task of creating a small dramatic scene showing people in different circumstances when the bombing started. They could be children or a family at home just going to bed; at work as firemen; workers just leaving work; hospital workers. Get them to write out their playscripts before performing to the rest of the class.
▶ Provide art materials for the children to create a frieze of background scenery for their dramas. They could show the bombing taking place, the fires and smoke, and so on.

Interview: Experiencing the Blitz

This interview with Megan Saxelby gives us a firsthand insight into the experiences of people who lived through the Second World War. She was 19 years old and at work when the war broke out and has vivid memories of what happened. Megan describes how dreadful it was during the bombing in Coventry. Every day there would be news of people killed and houses knocked down. She explains how people never knew what was going to happen next. Megan describes how her father made up the Anderson shelter at home, burying it in the garden, putting in steps and making the floor comfortable. The bombing was particularly bad in Coventry because the enemy were trying to hit the aircraft factories there, and Megan explains how the family would have to go down into the shelter every night.

She particularly remembers the horror she felt at the sound of the sirens. These became commonplace after August of 1940, when the worst of the Blitz began. She tells how street shelters had to be used if people happened to be out of the house when the sirens went off. The sirens were, for Megan, one of the most horrible memories she has, and she still feels dreadful when she hears them now, even if only on TV. She feels that the war changed everyone's lives and cites examples, such as how tired people were because they were usually up all night and how they had to carry gas masks all the time. She explains how she felt sympathy for German people who suffered the same things, but how in wartime people's feelings for others in other lands changed. Megan feels that one of the things that helped people in Britain to get through the war was the great influence of Winston Churchill.

Discussing the interview
▶ Watch and listen to the interview and repeat this if necessary, especially if there are EAL children in the class.
▶ Explain a little about Megan Saxelby and how the interview aims to explain what people's experiences during the war were like.
▶ Ask the children if they can remember the meaning of the word *Blitz*.
▶ Ask if anyone knows where Coventry is and talk about why this city was targeted by the Germans.
▶ Ask what the worst thing was that Megan remembered about the war.
▶ Discuss what shelters were, and why they were buried in the ground.
▶ Ask the children to recount how the war changed the lives of ordinary civilians.
▶ Discuss what it was that kept people going in the war.
▶ Introduce the term *propaganda* and discuss what this was.

Activities
▶ Use the word cards on photocopiable page 26 with the children, discussing the meanings of *air raid siren* and *air raid shelters*.
▶ Play the children the 'Air raid siren' (provided on the CD) and ask them to note down words to describe the feelings Megan must have experienced when she heard this sound. Challenge them to write a short piece of poetry about the sirens and how Megan, or other people, felt when they heard them going off.

▶ Show the children how to create a Powerpoint presentation on the computer and encourage them to begin to find out information about the bombing and the Blitz, and then to create slides for a presentation using their findings.
▶ Provide art materials for the children to paint pictures of what they think a town like Coventry might have looked like at night during the bombing. Discuss the colours and lights that would have been seen.

Dresden after the bombing

Following the bombing in Britain, and particularly as a result of the bombing of Coventry, which was very heavy, there was considerable anger amongst British civilians. This response, and the need to crush German civilian morale, led to Churchill's decision to carry out equally heavy bombing raids on German cities. This photograph shows Dresden following an air raid by British bombers in 1945. Some thought that the devastation caused was probably greater than in Britain, and have criticised Churchill for taking such a strong stance, especially since Dresden was not an industrial city, but a cultural centre. However, at the time, people in Britain were not sorry for what had been done because of their great hatred for their enemy.

Discussing the photograph
▶ Show the children the photograph and ask them what they think it shows. Ask them what has happened to the buildings.
▶ Explain that this is a photograph of Dresden, a German town, after being bombed by allied forces.
▶ Ask the children what buildings have been bombed. Discuss how, in fact, it is hard to find a single building that has not been damaged by a bomb.
▶ Ask the children to imagine what it must have been like in Dresden during the bombing.
▶ Talk about how the bombing was just as bad in Germany as it was in Britain. How do the children feel knowing that their country inflicted this damage on another country? Ask the children how they feel about any current conflict in the world, if appropriate.
▶ Talk with the children about how the German people must have feared British and American planes just as the British feared German ones.

Activities
▶ Explain to the class that Dresden was bombed in 1945, and help them to label this event on the timeline on photocopiable page 27. Note how this was right at the end of the war. Ask the children to consider whether it was a vengeful attack, since it came right at the end of the war, when it was not really a necessary thing to do in order for the Allies to win.
▶ Read the extract from 'The Silver Sword' (photocopiable page 30) extract to the children and talk about the experience of the Polish children in the story.
▶ Get the class to locate Dresden on a map of Europe or of Germany. Ask them to find a picture of modern-day Dresden on the Internet or in reference books, and to compare this image with the photograph.
▶ Challenge the children to write a ghost story or an adventure story, set in the ruins of Dresden shown in the photograph.
▶ Play the part of the interview 'Experiencing the Blitz' where Mrs Saxelby talks about how people in Britain felt about the bombing of Dresden at the time. Ask the children to write an account of news of the Dresden bombing from the point of view of a British person at the time.

Gas poster

In addition to dropping bombs, it was widely believed at the beginning of the war that German aeroplanes would be dropping gas over Britain. It was thought that lung irritants, sneezing gases and blister gases might be used. Consequently, measures were taken to provide everyone with gas masks, and it was ordered at the beginning of the war that they should be carried everywhere. Posters such as this one were put up to reinforce to people the importance of keeping gas masks with them and of wearing the mask as soon as there was an air-raid warning. Sometimes there would be false alarms and panic when someone thought they could smell gas, but in the end the Germans never used gas against the British civilian population.

Discussing the poster

▶ Ask the children to look carefully at the picture and tell you what it is (a warning poster or leaflet).

▶ Ask the children what kind of gas the poster is warning about.

▶ Look at the images that have been used on the poster, such as the appearance of gas falling onto the letter A and the double image of the person falling to the ground.

▶ Discuss how the figure has been drawn to create the appearance of being poisoned.

▶ Ask the children why they think these posters were used and why they were made to look so striking.

▶ Discuss the effectiveness of the poster – do the children think it is striking?

▶ Point out the limited use of colour and talk about why this was (to produce a bold effect and for economy).

Activities

See 'Children wearing gas masks', below.

Children wearing gas masks

All children had to wear gas masks at the beginning of the war, as adults did, due to the perceived fear of gas attacks by Germany. Children's masks were large and made to fit right over their heads for extra security. Children were also issued with Mickey Mouse gas masks with rubber ear pieces, in an attempt to encourage them to wear them. The large cardboard boxes around the children's necks were for carrying the masks. Unfortunately, most children did not like the masks, because of the way they looked with their large tin canisters at the bottom, and they did not like the rubbery smell when they were worn. Some said they felt it was difficult to breathe in them.

Discussing the photograph

▶ Ask the children what they think these small children are wearing.

▶ Discuss the reasons for children having to wear these masks.

▶ Ask the class if they can guess why the children all have boxes on strings around their necks.

▶ Ask what age they think the children in the photograph are.

▶ Ask if they think the children in the photograph would have felt excited or frightened when they had to put on their gas masks. What would they feel like if they had to wear them now?

Activities

▶ Compare what happened in the Second World War to what is happening in today in different parts of the world, such as Palestine, Israel, Kurdish Iraq, where people have been attacked with poisonous gases. Ask the children to look at the news and find out about places where there is a fear of gas attacks at the moment, possibly as a homework activity. Ask them to talk about their findings in school.

▶ Provide art materials with only a limited range of colours and ask the children to design a modern warning poster about gas attacks.

▶ Show the class the photograph 'Children wearing gas masks' and get the children to write down their first reactions. Do they think the children look humorous to them now? Why do they think this is? (The alien situation to the children's own experiences, the old-fashioned clothes.)

▶ Get the children to suggest a variety of adjectives to describe what it must have felt like to wear a gas mask. Make the list into a word bank for the children to use in writing imaginary descriptions of what it was like to put on a gas mask for the first time.

Evacuees

This photograph shows the arrival of children in south Wales. They were evacuees from the Midlands who had been sent to safety on special evacuation trains. The Midlands, as well as London, were also heavily bombed because of the large number of munitions factories in cities like Birmingham and Coventry. Children were sent away to safer, rural locations away from the bombing, but many were so unhappy that they soon returned home. Here we see the children being received from the train by adults known as billeting officers. The billeting officers would direct them to centres where they would be allocated to their new temporary homes, known as billets. Although people were as kind as it was possible to be in such circumstances, the children were often frightened and confused, this usually being the first time they had been away from home. The identity tags that the children wore can be seen tied around their necks, and their gas masks are also visible in the photograph.

Discussing the photograph

▶ Encourage the children to study the picture and ask what they particularly notice about it (the large number of children).

▶ Explain that the children in the photograph have arrived on a train from the Midlands to south Wales. Ask if the class know why they have all travelled to Wales and explain, if necessary, that they have been sent to avoid the dangers of the Blitz in the Midlands. Tell the children that they were called *evacuees*.

▶ Get the children to decide whether the evacuees seem happy, sad or have some other emotion on their faces.

▶ Talk about how many of these children had never been away from home before. Discuss how the places they went to seemed strange to them, as they were so different from the towns and cities they were used to.

▶ Tell the class that the children in this photograph were sent on their own, without their parents, to stay with strangers in their homes. How would the children feel if this happened to them? How do they think the evacuees felt?

▶ Ask the children to identify any particular things they notice about the evacuees in the photograph. Point out the identity labels and gas masks, explaining why these were necessary.

Activities

▶ Use the word cards on photocopiable page 25 to familiarise the children with evacuee terminology, such as *billets*, *identity tags*.

▶ Tell the children that you want them to act out a scene where evacuees are divided up and sent to their billets after arriving at their rural destination. Ask for volunteers to perform to a class direction. Use items such as identity labels and suitcases as props. Then encourage the children to think of some dialogue and to write a short playscript based on the scene.

▶ Use the extract 'The Silver Sword' (photocopiable page 30) and ask the children to write a similar story about having to leave home in the war.

▶ Read excerpts from *Goodnight Mr Tom* by Michelle Magorian (Longman) to the class and talk about the experiences of the evacuee in this story. Ask the children to write a reasoned argument about why children needed to be evacuated during the Blitz.

A ration book

During the war food quickly became scarce. Food became difficult to import and there were fewer people available to work on farms to continue the necessary food production. Although steps were taken to rectify these problems, such as the establishment of the Women's Land Army, it still became necessary to ration food supplies in an attempt to ensure everyone had their fair share. The ration book in this picture, issued in 1943, shows how the system worked. Everyone was allowed a certain amount of different types of food each week and the shopkeepers would mark the book once someone had collected their ration. It is interesting to note the lack of fresh fruit and vegetables marked in this book. During the war fruit was rarely seen by ordinary people, and they were expected to grow fresh vegetables for themselves in their gardens or allotments.

Discussing the photograph

▶ Look carefully at the picture with the class and ask them to explain what it shows. Get them to understand that it is a photograph of the cover of a ration book, on the left, and the pages from the inside of the book, on the right.

▶ Ask if anyone knows what a ration book is. When was it used? Give the children the relevant information, and ask if ration books are used today.

▶ Ask the children why they think that rationing was introduced during the war.

▶ Get the children to identify what kinds of food were available during the war, from the inside pages of the book.

▶ Ask the children what other kinds of food people needed, that are missing from the ration

book (fruit and vegetables). Can anyone suggest why these weren't available during the war?
▶ Can the children tell you who issued ration books?
▶ Tell the class that many other things were rationed, such as clothes. Explain how people had to save coupons before they 'bought' new clothes.
▶ Ask the children what they think happened to people who had lived on rationed food for five years (they became thinner). Can the children think of any other side effects of not eating a lot, or a variety of different foods (some nutrition was missing from people's diets)?

Activities
▶ Send out a note to the children's parents or carers some time before beginning this topic and ask for any old ration books to be loaned for the children to look at (they will need to be carefully recorded and stored safely).
▶ Give the children a copy of the 'Rationing allowance' sheet (photocopiable page 29). Bring in some of the items, such as sugar and tea, and let the children weigh these to get an idea of how much of each item people were allowed each week.
▶ Look at the list of items on the 'Rationing allowance' sheet. Ask the children to imagine eating only these things for a whole week. Talk about what meals could be made from them. Get them to draw a series of pictures or cartoons over a week, showing what meals they could make.

Make-do and mend poster

In addition to growing food at home, civilians in Britain were encouraged to be very thrifty in aid of 'the war effort'. Everyone was expected to make their possessions last as long as possible. When clothes began to wear out, people were expected to mend and patch them rather than go to the shops to buy new ones (which wasn't always an option as clothes were rationed and had to be bought with coupons that were saved up). All available clothing supplies had to be diverted into the making of uniforms for soldiers. People were also encouraged to make their own clothes, by sewing and knitting. Other household implements were expected to be reused for other purposes where possible. People were asked to hand in unwanted pots and pans, for instance, so that the metal could be used in making war machinery and ammunition.

Discussing the poster
▶ Look carefully at this picture with the class and ask them what kind of picture they think it is (a poster). Why do they think it was made?
▶ Discuss the main caption and what it means. Ask if the children have ever heard this saying before.
▶ Explain that it was a well-known saying during and some time after the war. Tell the children that items, such as clothes, were very scarce and people had to 'make-do' by mending the clothes that they had.
▶ Ask the children to suggest where the poster was put up. Explain this came from the government, and that the poster and the message needed to go out to everyone in the country, and so would have been put up across Britain.
▶ Focus on the two figures on the poster. Ask the children to suggest what each one signifies, and what sort of items each figure is suggesting can be mended. Explain how metal things were collected in and used for making machines and weapons, if the children don't understand what the metal figure represents.
▶ Talk about things that the children have at home that could be used for other purposes. For example, using shoe boxes to hold toys.
▶ Discuss why people were not expected to buy a lot of new clothes, or to give away pots and pans. Explain about the meaning of the phrase 'the war effort'.

Activities
▶ Bring in an assortment of household items and ask the children to discuss what they could have been used for during the war.
▶ Provide materials for the children to create their own poster about helping 'the war effort'.
▶ Challenge the children, working in pairs, to write down as many 'sayings' as they can think of related to saving or mending items, such as *Waste not want not*, *Look after the pennies and the pounds will look after themselves*.

Women factory workers

A major change that took place during the Second World War was the employment of women to do work that had been thought of as the preserve of men for many years. This photograph shows women working in a munitions factory making parts for Spitfire aeroplanes. This would certainly have been considered work only for men in the years before the war. However, the shortage of men to work in the factories at home enabled women to show their abilities for the first time in this kind of work, and also enabled them to contribute to the war effort. As the war progressed, the need for a work force on the home front resulted in the government conscripting unmarried women between 19 and 30 in December 1941. Women entered all sorts of work for the first time, becoming firewomen and ambulance drivers. Others joined the Auxiliary Territorial Service which was attached to the army, where they were trained as mechanics, clerks and anti-aircraft gun operators.

Discussing the photograph
▶ Ask the children what they think the women in the photograph are doing.
▶ Explain how many women went to work for the first time during the war, in factories and on farms, or driving lorries and buses. Discuss why this was.
▶ Get the children to think of all the jobs that needed doing in Britain during the war.
▶ Explain how before the war, it was not expected that women should do these jobs. Discuss the reasons for this and ask the children to suggest the things that women were allowed to do before the war.
▶ Explain that the photograph shows a munitions factory. Talk about the meaning of the word *munitions*. Can the children think why munitions needed to be produced and why the work was so important.
▶ Talk about the danger involved in doing this work (the risk of being bombed). Can the children suggest why these factories were in danger of being bombed?
▶ Do the children think the women in the photograph were brave? Why?

Activities
▶ Work together with the class to make a list of all the munitions that were made during the war. Get them to use reference books to look this information up, and to make illustrations of their findings.
▶ Locate on a map the major towns and cities where munitions factories were based. Give the children maps of Britain and ask them to mark the factories on them. Add these pieces of work to the children's books about the war.
▶ Give the children the beginning of a daily diary entry, written from the perspective of a munitions factory worker, and ask the children to complete it in their own words.
▶ Ask the children to write an account from the perspective of a female munitions worker during the war. Encourage them to consider the change in lifestyle and how this would have affected women's lives. They could conduct research prior to writing, if appropriate.

NOTES ON THE PHOTOCOPIABLE PAGES

Word cards
PAGE 24–6

A number of specific types of vocabulary have been introduced on the word cards:
▶ words associated with fighting the war, such as *the Blitz, air raid, Allies*
▶ words associated with evacuation, such as *evacuee, billets, identity tags*
▶ words associated with the home front, such as *gas masks* and *ration books.*
Encourage the children to think of other appropriate words to add to those on the word cards in order to build up a word bank for the topic.

Activities
▶ Encourage the children to summarise their learning at the end of the topic by composing sentences using key words from the word cards.
▶ Devise word games, such as crosswords, word searches or cloze procedure activities, using the word cards.

▶ Encourage the children to use the word cards in descriptive, factual and imaginative writing on the topic.

Timeline of the Second World War

PAGE 27

This timeline can be used to introduce children to the notion of chronology over a short, specific period of time. This timeline can be used effectively alongside the other resources in The Second World War Resource Gallery on the CD-ROM.

The timeline can be enlarged for class use by making it into a wall frieze. The kind of timeline shown here can also be useful at the end of a topic, for checking children's success in grasping ideas of sequence, chronology and, for those at that stage, understanding of the use of dates. The children could create their own version of the timeline, or could complete a blank, or partially completed, outline to add the events in the correct order and place pictures from the CD in the appropriate places on it.

Discussing the timeline

▶ Clarify with the children what the dates on the timeline mean and how long the span of time it covers is. Discuss why this timeline shows only a few years and yet is as long as others which show a great span of years.
▶ Point out the 'reading direction' of the timeline. Explain that as this represents the passing of time it is important to read it in the correct direction, and that it needs to be read from top to bottom.

Activities

▶ Suggest the children find other timelines in the class collection of books about the Second World War and use these to develop and add to their own copies of the timeline.
▶ Give the children a blank timeline and some key dates and information to fill in on it. (This will provide some useful assessment evidence.)
▶ Talk about key events and personalities during the period and ask the children to add more key events to the timeline as appropriate. They could also add photographs and other images from the Second World War Resource Gallery on the CD onto the correct parts of the timeline.

Blackout rules

PAGE 28

Rules like these were issued in every locality during the war. It was, of course, extremely important to ensure that no light from buildings or roads was visible to enemy bomber planes flying above, since this would have aided them in hitting their targets. Consequently, blackout rules were taken very seriously; they were a matter of life and death. The rules were enforced by the Air Raid Wardens, people from the local community who had to ensure people's safety during the raids. The rules show how people covered their doors and windows in their houses, and also how precautions had to be taken outside. They give us an indication of how strange it must have been at night in the streets, where everything would have been pitch dark. As a result of these strict, but necessary, precautions there were many traffic accidents. These dangers and the unpleasantness of living in the blackout are an aspect of life in the war that children can begin to appreciate through reading rules like these.

Discussing the text

▶ Read through the rules with the class and discuss what aspects of life they affected.
▶ Talk about how people were expected to follow them, for example by putting blankets at their windows, or covering their windows with newspaper. Explain how even the slightest chink of light was not allowed.
▶ Discuss what it must have been like to go out to the cinema or theatre at night with no street lights on.
▶ Discuss the dangers of having no lights in the streets.

Photograph © Corel

▶ Ask the children how they would feel in a situation with rules like these to abide by.
▶ Explain how the blackout probably added to the fear and stress of living in wartime.

Activities
▶ Ask the children to write a list of rules about how to save electricity today. For example, that computers may not be used in homes after 7pm.
▶ Divide the class into small groups to create a 'Blackout drama' which involves some kind of accident or serious incident as a result of following the blackout rules during the war.

Rationing allowance
PAGE 29

Food was very strictly rationed during the war so that everybody would have their fair share. With the increasing presence of enemy ships at sea and of submarine attacks, ships bringing supplies to Britain from other parts of the world found it increasingly difficult to get through. At first, most people tried to manage on their weekly ration, but soon they began to get hungry and they tried to get extra things. People who bought and sold extra food were said to be in the 'black market'. As the war dragged on, the black market grew more and more widespread. Many people who experienced this period talk about the many things they missed, such as luxury foods like sweets and chocolate, and imported fruits, such as bananas. Many types of fresh foods were largely unavailable unless you could grow them yourself or get them on the black market. Even eggs, for instance, were unavailable for much of the time, and people had to use powdered egg.

Discussing the text
▶ Read through the text with the class and ask them for their initial thoughts on it.
▶ Discuss what foods were available and the monotony of living on such limited rations.
▶ Explain the quantities of food to the class, pointing out what a small amount of each type there was.
▶ Get the children to think about certain types of food that are not included in the list, such as sweets, fruit. Discuss why they are not mentioned.
▶ Talk about the term 'black market' and ask the children to think about what this meant. Explain how very often people would pay extra for things on the black market, and how some people made a lot of money illegally from it.
▶ Discuss how people's diets affected them during the war. Do the children think they would be more or less healthy than people today?

Activities
▶ Challenge the children to work in pairs to find out further information from the Internet and reference books about living conditions during the war. They could work on different aspects of life, such as work, school, clothing, food.
▶ Create a role-play activity in which the children have to ensure that they all have a fair share. Set them a problem where there are not enough resources (of any kind) to go around and ask them to work in groups to come up with a solution. They will need to make a note of their solutions and talk to the class about their ideas at the end of the lesson.
▶ Set different groups the task of writing a wartime recipe using the ingredients listed in the text. They will need to write up cooking instructions as if the recipe were in a cookery book. Before starting the activity it will help to look at a few real recipes, so that the children can become familiar with their layout and content.

The Silver Sword
PAGE 30

This extract from *The Silver Sword* by Ian Serraillier gives a different perspective on the experiences of children during the Second World War. The story is set in Warsaw, where the Nazis have already occupied the area and have begun to take away civilians. The children in the story are caught up in this situation and the adventure is based on their efforts to avoid capture. The story is a useful one in that it shows that experiences differed depending on circumstances during the war. Children in many parts of Europe had much more dangerous, frightening experiences than their peers in Britain. Although the suffering of children caught up in the Blitz was terrible, children will also learn from this extract that the fear and horror experienced by people in Europe was considerably worse in some ways.

Discussing the story

▶ Read through the introductory paragraph and the extract with the class and discuss the situation that the children are in.

▶ Explain that they live in Warsaw, and talk about where this is.

▶ Tell the class that many Jewish families lived and worked in Poland at this time. Explain that the Nazis were attempting to restrict the lives of the Jews in Europe, and even to expel them from their homes or kill them. Talk about the labour camps and concentration camps that the Jews were sent to, and discuss what happened to many people who were sent there.

▶ Discuss how dangerous this really was for any children caught up in the situation.

▶ Ask the class why they think the children's parents in the story have been taken away.

▶ Discuss the meaning of the term *storm troopers*.

▶ Ask the class why they think the children have decided they must escape.

▶ Discuss what happened to the children's home as soon as they had left it.

▶ Ask the class to think what the children might do next.

Activities

▶ Challenge the children to write the next incident in the story themselves.

▶ Read the rest of the book with the class, or encourage the children to read it themselves.

▶ Arrange for two or three children who have read the story to take the hot seat and answer questions posed by the rest of the class about their experiences during the war.

Second World War word cards

the Blitz

air raid

bomb damage

Allies

Axis

Evacuation word cards

host family

evacuee

billets

billeting officer

identity tags

Home front word cards

gas masks

ration books

air raid siren

air raid shelters

blackout

◣SCHOLASTIC
PHOTOCOPIABLE

Timeline of the Second World War

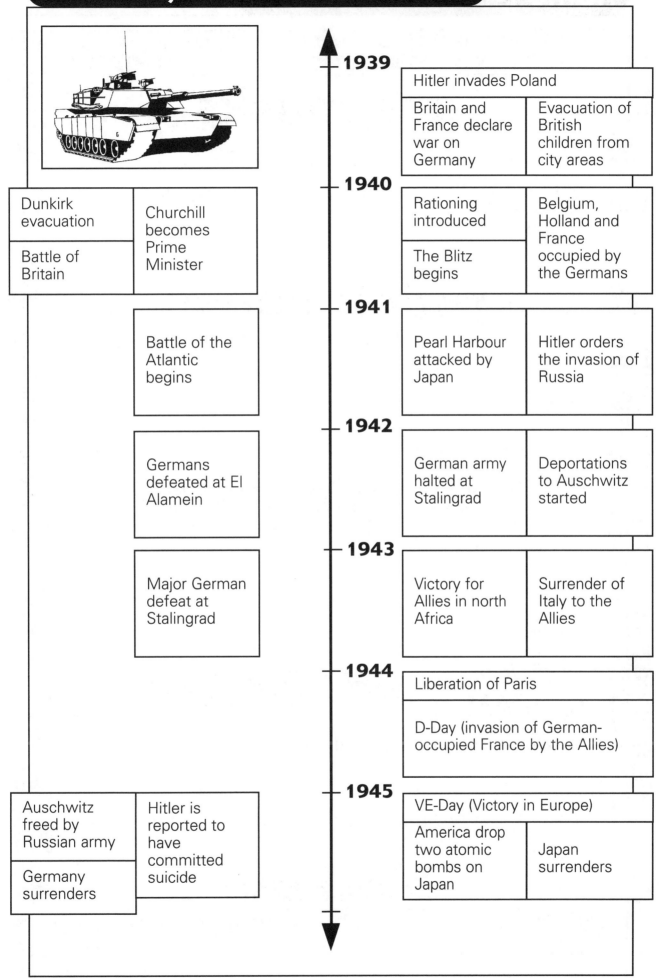

1939

Hitler invades Poland

| Britain and France declare war on Germany | Evacuation of British children from city areas |

1940

Dunkirk evacuation

Churchill becomes Prime Minister

Battle of Britain

| Rationing introduced | Belgium, Holland and France occupied by the Germans |
| The Blitz begins | |

1941

Battle of the Atlantic begins

| Pearl Harbour attacked by Japan | Hitler orders the invasion of Russia |

1942

Germans defeated at El Alamein

| German army halted at Stalingrad | Deportations to Auschwitz started |

1943

Major German defeat at Stalingrad

| Victory for Allies in north Africa | Surrender of Italy to the Allies |

1944

Liberation of Paris

D-Day (invasion of German-occupied France by the Allies)

1945

VE-Day (Victory in Europe)

Auschwitz freed by Russian army

Hitler is reported to have committed suicide

Germany surrenders

| America drop two atomic bombs on Japan | Japan surrenders |

Blackout rules

All windows and doors in houses must be completely covered with heavy black curtains, blinds, blankets or newspaper, so that no light shows through outside.

Shops, pubs, theatres and all other public buildings must ensure no light shows at night from windows or doors.

No torches are allowed to be used outside except in emergencies, when their beams must be pointed down towards the ground.

Street lights will be turned off at night.

Traffic lights and car lights must be shaded with hoods or discs to reduce the beam on the road, and vehicles must not travel at more than 30mph.

There must be blinds on the windows of buses and trains.

SCHOLASTIC
PHOTOCOPIABLE

Rationing allowance

A weekly ration that one person could buy using their ration book normally included the following:

1oz of tea

8oz of sugar

8oz of butter or other fat

1oz of cheese

4oz of bacon or ham

1 shilling and 2 pence worth of meat

Note

1 shilling and 2 pence = approximately 8 new pence
1oz = 25gms

The Silver Sword

This extract is about the escape of three children, Edek, Bronia and Ruth, from their home in Warsaw, when it is attacked by Nazi storm troopers. The children's parents have already been taken away by the soldiers and the children are now in danger themselves. Here, they are attempting to escape over the roof.

The first few steps – as far as the V between the chimney and the roof ridge – were ghastly. Edek made a dash for it, grabbed the telephone bracket and hauled himself up, with Bronia clinging on behind. She was speechless with terror. He reached back and hauled Ruth up after him.

After a few moments' rest, they slid down a few feet on to a flat part that jutted out, a sort of parapet.

The roof ridge lay between them and the street, so they could not see what was happening down there. But they could hear shouting, the whine of cars, the screech of brakes.

Luckily for them, all the houses on this side of the school were joined together in one long terrace, otherwise they could not have got away. Even so, it was a miracle that none of their slips and tumbles ended in disaster.

They must have gone fully a hundred yards when the first explosion shook the air. A sheet of fire leapt up from their home into the frosty night sky. They fell flat in the snow and lay there. The roof shook, the whole city seemed to tremble. Another explosion. Smoke and flames poured from the windows. Sparks showered into the darkness.

"Come along," said Edek. "We shan't let them have us now."

With growing confidence they hurried along the roof-tops. At last, by descending a twisted fire escape, they reached street level. On and on they hurried, not knowing or caring where they went so long as they left those roaring flames behind them.

They did not stop till the fire was far away and the pale winter dawn was breaking.

They took shelter in the cellar of a bombed house. Exhausted, huddled together for warmth, they slept till long after midday, when cold and hunger woke them.

© Ian Serraillier

ANCIENT EGYPT

Content, skills and concepts

This chapter relates to Unit 10 of the QCA Scheme of Work for history at Key Stage 2, 'What can we find out about Ancient Egypt from what has survived?'. It is assumed that this unit will be taught mainly to Years 3 or 4, but it could also be adapted for teaching to children in older age groups. In conjunction with the Ancient Egypt Resource Gallery on the CD-ROM, this chapter aims to support teachers in dealing with images of artefacts, ancient sites and excavations from the Ancient Egyptian civilisation, and in teaching about the lives and beliefs of people from different levels of Ancient Egyptian society.

Recounting stories about the past, and looking for similarities and differences between the past and the present, are prior learning activities which will have introduced useful skills and concepts to the children before they progress to learning about this topic. This chapter includes suggestions for the extension of these and other skills, particularly the interpretation and analysis of historical sources.

Resources on the CD-ROM

The Ancient Egypt Resource Gallery ranges from maps and photographs to illustrations and narratives. The Resource Gallery also provides materials to support the teaching of key historical concepts, such as source analysis and interpretation relevant to this period and theme. These resources include a map, illustrations and photographs of artefacts and historical sites.

Photocopiable pages

Photocopiable resources can be accessed within the book and are also provided in PDF format on the CD-ROM, from which they can be printed. These include:
▶ word and sentence cards which highlight the essential vocabulary of this topic
▶ a timeline
▶ examples of hieroglyphics
▶ fiction and non-fiction texts
▶ a writing frame
The teacher's notes in this chapter include suggestions for developing discussion when using the sheets and ways of using them for whole class, or for group or individual activities.

Texts

The stories and accounts attempt to introduce children to an ancient way of life very different from their own, and to interest them in a past civilisation. Texts include fiction and non-fiction writing and also introduce children to an ancient type of script. The texts have been written at different reading levels.

History skills

This chapter draws out skills in the children such as observing, describing, using time-related vocabulary, sequencing, using a timeline, understanding the meaning of dates and key vocabulary, comparing, inferring, listening, speaking, reading, writing and drawing. For example, there is an opportunity for children to develop independent skills in sequencing through the use of a timeline which outlines the key events of the period. Children can learn to use descriptive vocabulary to describe the photographs included on the CD. They can conduct further research leading on from discussions about photographs, compiling notes on which to base a short speech delivered to their classmates.

Historical understanding

An overarching aim is for children to begin to develop a more detailed knowledge of the past through their understanding of the context and content of the factual information they use. They will begin to give reasons for events, use sources to find further information and be able to recount and rewrite stories and accounts they have heard, using different forms of presentation. They will also have the opportunity to extend their skills in using descriptive language and specific time-related terms in beginning to write their own factual accounts of the past.

NOTES ON THE CD-ROM RESOURCES

Map of Ancient Egypt

This map shows Ancient Egypt in the period between around 1600 and 1069BC. The whole of Upper and Lower Egypt and the major settlements are included. What the map principally shows very clearly is the way settlements were established along the course of the River Nile. This was due, not only to the supply of water provided by the river to water crops, but also because of the fertile soil in the flood plain of the river. The mud and silt washed down by the river waters provided excellent arable land for the early Egyptian farmers. Certain areas, such as those around Giza and Thebes, can be seen to be more heavily settled over a considerable area. Sinai marks the area now covered by the desert. Nubia was a separate African kingdom, and raids took place between the two kingdoms.

Discussing the map
▶ Ask the children what they already know about Ancient Egypt. Tell them how Egypt is an ancient country, and how Egyptian civilisation has existed for many thousands of years.
▶ Ask the children what they particularly notice about the shape and area of land covered by Ancient Egypt on the map. Point out how the settlements lie along the River Nile. Ask volunteers to suggest why the country grew into this shape and size.
▶ See if the children can identify any major cities, or sites, such as Thebes (Luxor), Abu Simbel or Giza.
▶ Point out how Egypt was for some time in two parts, Upper and Lower Egypt, and explain how it finally united to take over Nubia.

Activities
▶ Help the children to locate Egypt on a modern map or globe of the world. Ask the children what the most noticeable features are of modern Egypt (the sea coasts, the River Nile, the desert). Then compare this with the 'Map of Ancient Egypt', and point out how the same features as in modern times are still visible on the map.
▶ Use the word cards on photocopiable page 49 to encourage the children to use time-related vocabulary when discussing maps of Egypt, such as *ancient* and *modern*.
▶ Give the children their own copy of the map, and as they work through the topic get them to draw small illustrations of each place or site that they learn about.
▶ Explain to the children about the reasons for settlement along the banks of the Nile (proximity to the water and fertile soil). Provide materials for the children to carry out experiments growing seeds in different soils – dry, sandy and moistened soils – and to compare the growth of their seeds in each.
▶ Ask the children to search further into farming methods in Ancient Egypt, such as irrigation and the use of the shaduf (a device to lift water from the river).

The Valley of the Kings

The Valley of the Kings is a narrow valley on the west bank of the Nile, beyond the cliffs of the Theban Hills. It contains tombs that were cut into the rock face. This was one of the most sacred places to be buried for Ancient Egyptians and it has been found to contain the tombs of many of the later pharaohs, including Tutankhamun. By the early 20th century, over 60 tombs had been discovered and opened, including those of Seti I and II, Rameses I, II, III, VI and IX. Recently, an entire village built for the tomb workers has been discovered nearby. The tombs were decorated with paintings of scenes about the afterlife and were also filled with treasures and other items which the dead pharaoh would need in the afterlife.

Discussing the photograph
▶ Ask the children to look closely at the photograph and explain what they can see (tall cliffs, a pathway).
▶ Ask if anyone has ever visited this place, and get them to describe their experiences if they have.
▶ Explain that this is part of a long narrow valley, known as the Valley of the Kings. Ask if anyone can work out why it may have been given this name, and use questioning to guide

them, such as *Does it look like a place where people lived?* Explain that it was a very sacred place for the Ancient Egyptians, and that many of their most important pharaohs were buried here during the period of time known as the New Kingdom.

▶ Talk about the famous kings of the New Kingdom who were buried in the Valley of the Kings, such as Rameses I and II, and Seti I and II. Explain that the tomb of Tutankhamun was found here also.

▶ Ask the children to imagine what is must be like to walk in this valley, and discuss what the atmosphere must be like.

▶ Can the children suggest why this place was chosen by the pharaohs as their burial place? (It was calm, quiet and very impressive.)

Activities
See 'The antechamber of Tutankhamun's tomb', below.

The antechamber of Tutankhamun's tomb

The two photographs show two views of the antechamber of Tutankhamun's tomb, in the Valley of the Kings, as it was when it was first discovered in 1922. The tomb was discovered by the archaeologist, Sir Howard Carter, and its contents are considered an important collection, since many items from other pharaonic tombs were lost to tomb robbers. Tutankhamun, who ruled from about 1334 to 1325, is thought to have been murdered at the age of eighteen, and was probably fairly insignificant as a pharaoh. However, his tomb is one of the richest ever discovered. When Carter first discovered the antechamber, he peered through the hole he had made in the sealed doorway and was awestruck at the sight. The antechamber was piled high with hundreds of objects. All the items appeared to have been stacked into a space that was really too small for them, and possibly in some haste. Of all the objects in the antechamber, the chariots were perhaps the most important for archaeologists, since until this discovery only two chariots had been found. These were complete and of a most sophisticated kind, some probably used for hunting and others for 'state' occasions, decorated with gold, glass and precious stones. Carter found that the tomb had been opened twice, hundreds of years earlier, before he discovered it. The tomb had been re-sealed and although it had probably been robbed, as most of the tombs had been, very little had been taken.

Photograph 1
Two life-sized painted wooden figures of the king can be seen at the back of the photograph and parts of chariots. There is also an animal couch on the left of the photograph. Boxes and chests can be seen crammed into the room.

Photograph 2
Among the most interesting objects to be discovered included couches in the shape of animals – two can be seen on the right-hand side of the photograph. This view of the antechamber also shows the numerous boxes, chests, stools and chairs.

Discussing the photographs
▶ Ask the children if they can suggest what these photographs show.

▶ Explain to the class that the photographs were taken in the antechamber of Tutankhamun's tomb, when the first archaeologist, Howard Carter, found it.

▶ Ask if any of the children can tell you what an antechamber is (a room which is adjacent to the main room in the site and which is entered before going into this main room).

▶ Find volunteers to look at the photographs and identify some of the things that Carter found in the antechamber.

▶ Discuss how well preserved everything appears to be.

▶ Discuss with the children why all these things were in the tomb. Talk about the Ancient Egyptians' belief in the afterlife and how they thought that the dead pharaoh would need all his things there.

▶ Talk about the value of all these finds in Ancient Egypt to historians (the different kinds of chariots used by Tutankhamun had never been seen before, for example). Explain how the things in the photographs added to historian's knowledge of what life was like in Ancient Egypt, and that the items are valuable historical sources.

Activities

▶ Help the class locate the New Kingdom on the timeline (photocopiable page 53), and also to locate the Valley of the Kings on the 'Map of Ancient Egypt' (provided on the CD).

▶ Ask the children to write a descriptive passage or a poem to describe the atmosphere in the Valley of the Kings or the feelings of an archaeologist uncovering a tomb for the first time.

▶ Provide the children with resources, such as books and the Internet, so they can carry out their own research into the work of Howard Carter and the discoveries he made in the tomb of Tutankhamun.

▶ Read the account 'Howard Carter's discoveries' (photocopiable page 55) with the children, up to the point where Carter discovers the antechamber.

▶ Provide materials for the children to make their own class book about Ancient Egypt.

▶ Look together at the timeline (photocopiable page 53) and consider how long all these things had been in the tomb before Carter discovered them.

Tomb of Tutankhamun

This photograph shows the figure of Tutankhamun still inside its sarcophagus (stone coffin). The sarcophagus was very securely buried in many different layers to protect it. When Howard Carter finally managed to enter the burial chamber itself, beyond the antechamber, he found that the golden shrine of Tutankhamun took up nearly all the space in the room. The first outer shrine was removed, only to reveal three further shrines, all carefully fitted one inside the other. The sarcophagus shown here was inside the smallest shrine, and was carved from a single block of quartzite, with a red granite lid.

Inside the sarcophagus was a set of three coffins, once again all carefully fitted one inside the other. Inside the third and smallest coffin, made entirely of gold, was Tutankhamun's mummy. The solid gold mask covering the mummy's face (see 'Funeral mask of Tutankhamun', below) was the most striking object. Unfortunately, a lot of the body had disintegrated, as the embalming oils that had been used had reacted badly with each other. He was found with a large number of rings on the remaining fingers, and with bracelets, amulets and earrings.

The wall paintings seen here are the only ones in the complex. The pictures on the left show the lower part of the west wall, where 12 baboon-deities sit. These symbolise the hours of the night through which the sun and the king must travel before arriving in the underworld. Behind the sarcophagus is the north wall, where the painting shows Tutankhamun, followed by his 'ka' or spiritual double, being welcomed into the underworld by Osiris, king of the dead. On the right can be seen the goddess Nut. On the same wall can be seen the opening of the mouth ceremony by Ay, Tutankhamun's successor, in which the deceased king's senses are restored.

Discussing the photograph

▶ Look closely at this photograph and ask the children what they think it shows. Explain that it is the burial chamber of Tutankhamun found by Howard Carter, next to the antechamber.

▶ Explain how this is one of the photographs Carter had taken when the excavation was in progress. Discuss why he decided to do this (to keep a record of exactly how things looked and where they were placed). Discuss why this could be important (the positioning of an object could have meant something special to the Ancient Egyptians).

▶ Study the wall paintings with the class, and discuss what they show and what they were intended to represent.

▶ Ask the children if they know what a sarcophagus is. Explain that it is made of solid stone, and that the coffin is inside it.

▶ Ask the children to look at the

Photograph © Photodisc, Inc.

sarcophagus itself and note the ornamentation on it. Focus on the winged goddesses carved on its sides and ask them to suggest why they have been added (to protect the body of the dead pharaoh).

Activities
See activities for 'Coffin' and 'Mummy', below.

Coffin

This photograph shows the coffin and mummy cover of Iyneferty, wife of Sennedjem (a workman), dated within the New Kingdom, around 1279 to 1213BC. The goddess Nut spreads her wings over the centre of the cover to the coffin (on the left of the photograph) in a protective gesture. The coffin was found at Thebes and is an example of fine craftsmanship.

The picture shows what would be seen when the lid of a coffin was first removed. To the right of the coffin cover there appears to be an inner coffin, designed to look like Iyneferty as she was in life. Inside the inner coffin, the body itself would have been placed, wrapped in layers of bandages. The mask covering the face would have been made to resemble that of the deceased person. Here, we see the hairstyle and jewellery and hair fastenings that she would have worn in life. In fact, the design on the inner coffin has the appearance of a living person.

Mummy

This photograph shows what is seen when the mummy inside the coffin is finally unwrapped. Although considerably shrunken, the body is clearly discernible. The skeleton, teeth and skin are all present, and in some cases, even the hair remains. The inner organs would have been removed by the embalmer, so that the body could be preserved, and these would have been buried in the tomb in canopic jars. The brain was removed through the nostrils with a spiked instrument, but the heart was left in the body. The empty body cavity and skull were then packed with preservatives – linen and aromatic herbs were used – to prevent any decay from taking place. The skin of the body in the photograph appears blackened, but this is likely to have been caused by the application of the substances applied to the body, which included embalming oils, perfumes, natron (salt) and molten resin, to dry the corpse. Often good luck charms were placed between the layers of bandages that the body was wrapped in after it had dried out. The mummification process took many weeks to complete.

Discussing the photographs
▶ Explain that these two photographs, along with the sarcophagus in the photograph 'Tomb of Tutankhamun', show all the different layers in which the body of a dead person was buried. There would be a stone tomb, several coffins in the form of the dead person, and inside the last coffin, the body itself, wrapped in bandages and mummified. Ask the children why they think the Ancient Egyptians did this (to preserve the body for its journey into the afterlife).
▶ Ask why the body had to be mummified, and explain the Egyptian belief in the afterlife. Explain that the body needed to remain intact so that it could go forward into the afterlife.
▶ Point out the images of gods and goddesses, some with wings spread, on the coffins in both the photographs, and ask the children why the Ancient Egyptians thought this was important (it was a sign that the gods would protect the deceased person).
▶ Look at the photograph of the coffin and discuss how we know this is the coffin of a woman (because of the hair and face on the mask).
▶ Point out the tiny figures to the children in the 'Coffin' photograph, and explain that these were called *shabti*. The shabti were small wooden figures which were placed in the tombs of those buried in the period of the New Kingdom. One view is that they represented the spirit of the dead person and accompanied them on their journey into the afterlife, working on their behalf. Other historians think that shabtis were figures of slaves who would go into the afterlife and work for the dead person.
▶ Discuss briefly the process of mummification with the children, explaining the removal of the internal organs, which were preserved and put into canopic jars, the preserving of the body with special salts, perfumes and oils, and the wrapping of the body in bandages. Explain how both the coffin containing the body and the canopic jars containing the internal organs were buried in the tomb, along with the possessions of the dead person and their shabtis.

Activities

▶ Help the children locate the period of Tutankhamun on the timeline on photocopiable page 53. Discuss the date when Howard Carter opened Tutankhamun's tomb, and note the expanse of time that had elapsed.

▶ Show the children the 'Map of Ancient Egypt' and the photograph 'The Valley of the Kings' (provided on the CD) to place in context where Tutankhamun's tomb was found. Point out how he was a very young pharaoh, who was not very famous, but that his tomb was richer than any others discovered, which is why it is so well known now. Discuss why this may have been, and ask the children to write a short discussion, putting down their reasons for the richness of his burial. Allow them to conduct further research if appropriate.

▶ Show the children the photograph of the 'Funeral mask of Tutankhamun' (provided on the CD), and point out that this mask was found in the tomb shown here and that it covered the face of Tutankhamun's mummy.

▶ If possible, organise a visit to a museum containing Ancient Egyptian artefacts, where the children can see, discuss and sketch them.

▶ Encourage the children to learn the key vocabulary when discussing this theme of Ancient Egyptian belief in life after death, by using the word cards on photocopiable pages 51 and 52.

▶ Encourage the children to carry out further research into the religious beliefs of the Ancient Egyptians and also their practices. They can include their work in a class book about Ancient Egypt, or use their work to create a classroom display.

▶ Provide bright paints and large sheets of paper for the children to make full-sized paintings of a pharaoh's coffin.

Funeral mask of Tutankhamun

This mask is part of a very important collection of funerary items from the tomb of Tutankhamun, which is held in the Egyptian Museum in Cairo. Tutankhamun lay inside this inner coffin in the funeral mask shown in the photograph. This mask is, perhaps, one of the greatest treasures ever found from Ancient Egypt. It weighs around 9 kilograms, and is made from two sheets of gold and has lapis lazuli and cornelian in it. Along with its beauty, the mask also served to preserve the king's face.

Discussing the photograph

▶ Ask the children if they have ever seen this object before. If not, discuss what it is and where it was found.

▶ Explain how Tutankhamun's tomb had been difficult to find, and how it had, therefore, been protected from tomb robbers who had taken most things from other tombs.

▶ Tell the children about the young pharaoh, Tutankhamun, for whom the mask was made.

▶ Ask volunteers to work out what the mask was made from and see if they can guess

▶ Talk about the reasons for the use of this mask (as a covering for the face of the dead king, to help Tutankhamun's spirit recognise his body in the afterlife).

▶ Talk briefly with the children about the beliefs of the Ancient Egyptians, and how they believed the body of the dead person must be preserved so that their spirits could live on in the afterlife (see the notes on 'The Book of the Dead', below).

Activities

▶ Ask the children to conduct research into the work of Howard Carter, focusing on his uncovering of Tutankhamun's tomb.

▶ Read the account 'Howard Carter's discoveries' (photocopiable page 55) with the children, focusing on the latter half of the text where Carter discovers the burial chamber.

▶ Get the children to make papier mâché masks or models of Tutankhamun based on this photograph.

Scarab pectoral necklace

This photograph shows the pectoral necklace that would have been worn in life and also laid on the chest of the mummy of the dead owner. This pectoral necklace is from the tomb of the Pharaoh Psusennes, who lived between 1039 and 991BC, and is now kept in the Egypt Museum in Cairo. The central image on the ornament is that of the winged scarab beetle, which was the symbol of the god of the rising sun. The scarab was important to Ancient

Egyptians, and it was revered as the cross is by Christians today. The scarab on the necklace in the photograph is supported by oval shapes, known as cartouches, bearing the name of the king. Cartouches were oval shapes which contained symbols representing the name of the Pharaoh. The cartouches are flanked by kneeling figures. Images such as the scarab were associated with kingship, and with the wish for protection and a successful journey into the afterlife. The necklace is richly made, with a gold base, semi-precious stones and coloured glass, showing not only the great wealth of the Egyptian pharaohs but also their desire to be cared for even in death.

Gold bracelet

This photograph shows a gold bracelet from the tomb of the Pharaoh Amenemope, who ruled between 993 and 984BC. There are gold solar discs that can be seen above the two main cartouches. These cartouches contain hieroglyphic writing, bearing the names of a pharaoh. These hieroglyphs give the names of the king's predecessor, Psusennes I. Once again the image of the scarab beetle, which represented the sun god and was important to the Ancient Egyptians, can be seen on the left-hand cartouche. The bracelet was made in two hinged halves and is set with intricate and elegant detailed patterns. The images of the scarab and the reference to the sun god convey the importance of the wearer of the bracelet, since they allude to kingship.

Discussing the photographs

▶ Look at the photograph 'Scarab pectoral necklace' and explain to the children what it is. Ask them to study the details carefully, and then ask for volunteers to point out the things they can recognise.
▶ Talk about the scarab beetle and its significance to the Ancient Egyptians.
▶ Ask the children if they know what the oval shapes are called (cartouches) and what they represent.
▶ Discuss the materials from which the necklace was made.
▶ Tell the children that the pectoral necklace would have been worn around the neck, with the main ornament on the chest, both in life and in death as a mummy.
▶ Look at the photograph of the 'Gold bracelet' and ask the children what they think it is made of.
▶ Explain to the children where the bracelet was found. Ask for volunteers to identify some of the images on the bracelet, and discuss their meaning and significance together.
▶ Discuss with the children the Ancient Egyptians' purpose of putting necklaces and bracelets onto mummies.

Activities

▶ Ask the children to look up other items of jewellery worn by Ancient Egyptians in life and which were placed on their mummies in their tombs. They could look at pictures of mummies on the Internet or in reference books.
▶ Provide art materials for the children to make an observational drawing of either the bracelet or the necklace from the photographs. They could use oil pastels or acrylic paint to add colour to their drawings.
▶ Challenge the children to write a careful explanation of why items, such as necklaces and bracelets were placed on mummies in their tombs. If they have studied other ancient cultures, such as the Anglo-Saxons or Vikings, they could make brief comparisons with their beliefs and practices.

A queen's furniture

The items of furniture seen in the photograph are the remains of what belonged to the wife of Sneferu, Hetepheres. Found in her tomb were a bed, a bed canopy, two armchairs and several chests. Here we see the bed and one of the armchairs, framed by the bed canopy. Dating from around 2613 to 2494BC, they show what elegant and expensive styles were favoured by the families of the ancient pharaohs. The fittings are made of copper and sheet gold, with golden inlays. They show the wealth, style and elegance of the lives of these families, but above all they show how advanced and comfortable life in these very early civilisations could be.

Discussing the photograph

▶ Look at the photograph with the children and discuss what the objects in it are.

▶ Ask the children how they can locate that they are from Ancient Egypt (the style, the headrest on the bed).

▶ Note the details of the furniture, such as the copper and sheet gold fittings.

▶ Can the children suggest what status of Egyptian this furniture belonged to? Explain where the items were found and to whom they belonged. Discuss how it would only have been very important people who would have had furniture in their homes like this.

▶ Talk about how queens and other important women were considered equally as important as men in Ancient Egypt. They could become rulers in their own right or have a great deal of power as mothers or relatives of the pharaoh.

▶ Ask the children if they think this furniture looks very different from modern furniture.

Activities

▶ Give the children a copy of the timeline on photocopiable page 53 and help them find the period when this type of furniture was made.

▶ Discuss why items like this were put into the tomb of a dead queen, and ask the children to write a list of all the things that they think a queen might want in her tomb to take her to the afterlife.

▶ Ask the children to compare these items of furniture with their modern-day equivalents, and to make a list of the similarities and differences. They could find other examples of old and modern furniture from reference books or magazines. They could then make a chart of their pictures, to show the comparisons between the old and the new.

Headdress

This headdress is typical of the styles seen in images of significant figures from Ancient Egypt. The detail and richness of its design are striking and it would no doubt have been very impressive as part of its owner's costume. It is thought to have belonged to a queen or lady of noble birth of the court of the pharaoh Thuthmosis III, and was found in the tomb of one of his Syrian wives. Made of gold, glass and semi-precious stones, it is thought to date from around 1469 to 1436BC. In the photograph the headdress is mounted on a modern wig made in the style of the period. Each small part of the headdress is joined to the next by a hinge, making the whole headdress flexible and able to bend and move with the movements of the wearer's head.

Discussing the photograph

▶ Explain to the children that this is an Ancient Egyptian headdress which has been displayed on a modern model with a modern wig. Tell them that the wig is in the style of the period, however.

▶ Get them to study the photograph closely, and identify how the headdress is made and what each piece is made from.

▶ Explain how each small piece has a hinge to join it to the next one. Can the children suggest why this was?

▶ Talk about the style of the headdress and how it resembles the shape of Egyptian women's hairstyles.

▶ Discuss what it must have felt like to wear the headdress. Can the children suggest what it might have felt like? (It was probably quite heavy.)

▶ Ask the children to suggest what sort of people would have worn a headdress like this in Ancient Egypt and ask them to give reasons for their suggestions.

Activities

▶ Help the children to locate the date of the headdress on the timeline on photocopiable page 53.

▶ Challenge the children to design their own headdress. They could research Ancient Egyptian clothing and make their design different to this one if they want to, comparing the different styles worn by the Egyptians.

▶ Provide pieces from constructional toys, such as Meccano, and ask the children to work in small groups to experiment with hinges, to find out how pieces of metal move when hinged together. They could then give a verbal explanation to other groups.

Papyrus

This photograph shows what papyrus looks like when growing in its natural state. Papyrus is a tall reed, which the Ancient Egyptians found to be useful in making paper. The long stems were split open and cut into thin strips and flattened out. They were then placed close together, side by side, and more were laid on top at right angles. The whole was flattened and left to dry under a weight. The sap oozing out from the reeds made the layers stick together to make a sheet which could then be written on. Many original papyrus scrolls have survived from Ancient Egyptian times, preserved due to the dry climate of Egypt. The hieroglyphics on them have been translated and have allowed historians to discover invaluable information about life then. Scribes used scrolls to record information such as the amount of tax that people had to pay, the amount of materials being used in workshops, such as paint, or for writing reports on (one report survives from 1100bc recording tomb robberies in Thebes).

Discussing the photograph
▶ Ask the children what they think this photograph shows. Can anyone suggest what the plants are called? Point out that they are growing along the river banks and see if this clue helps them.
▶ Talk about papyrus with the children and explain how it was made into paper if no one can tell you.
▶ Explain how 'paper' in Ancient Egypt was referred to as *papyrus*. Tell the children that a great deal of papyrus was made by the Ancient Egyptians and ask the children what they think it was used for.

Activities
▶ Write the word *papyrus* on the board and ask the children if it reminds them of a word in English that we use today. Point out how the word *paper* is derived from it. Ask the children if they can think of any other words in use today that could be derived from Ancient Egyptian words.
▶ Ask the children to carry out further research of their own into papyrus and what it was used for. Ask them to turn their research into a summarised paragraph, ensuring the main points they have found out are covered.
▶ Ask the children to write their own set of instructions for making papyrus.

The Book of the Dead

This photograph shows a small section from the Book of the Dead. It was found in the burial place of Nakhte, an important scribe, who probably scribed this book. The book was written between about 1550 and 1300bc. This book, made from papyrus, contained a collection of about 200 magic spells, written to make the journey to the afterlife safer for the spirit of the dead person. Some spells were written to protect the person, from demons, for example. In the scene shown here, the dead man and his wife are shown standing in a garden, surrounded by trees and date palms. In front of them, and from a different perspective, is a pool surrounded by trees. In the background is a house, built on a platform to protect it from damp and from the regular flooding which took place on the banks of the Nile. The man and women are standing before the god Osiris. Hieroglyphics can be seen in the background. The eventual discovery of how to read hieroglyphics in the 19th century meant that much could be learned from sources like this about the beliefs and practices of the Ancient Egyptians. Many Books of the Dead were produced en masse in places called Houses of Life, written there by priests and scribes.

Discussing the photograph
▶ Look carefully at the photograph with the class and ask them to tell you what it shows. Can anyone point out the details in the picture?
▶ Explain that it is a part of a book called the Book of the Dead, and that it was made on papyrus.
▶ Talk about why it was called by this name and explain its purpose to the class.
▶ Discuss with the children why the Ancient Egyptians thought there was a need for a book of magic spells.
▶ Discuss who the people drawn in the book might be, and what they might be doing (they

are probably the people who have died and they are seen being protected by the god Osiris, king of the dead).

▶ Discuss the way different perspectives are used in the picture, for example the people are seen from the side, while the pool is seen from above. Why do the children think the picture was drawn in this way? (It was a particular style of the Egyptians as they did not know how to represent things in other ways.)

▶ Talk about who might have made this Book of the Dead, for example a scribe. Talk about the meaning of the word *scribe*.

Activities

See 'Hieroglyphics', below.

Hieroglyphics

These very decorative hieroglyphics were found on the coffin of Petosiris. They date from the Ptolemaic period, just prior to the imposition of Roman rule in Egypt. The text used is copied from Chapter 42 of a Book of the Dead. The word *hieroglyphics*, meaning 'sacred carvings', was given to Egyptian script by the Ancient Greeks. Hieroglyphics were used for about 3, 500 years, until about AD400 when they died out. It is also at this time that the record of Ancient Egyptian history ends. This history would have been lost had it not been for the discovery of the Rosetta Stone. This broken fragment of stone, discovered by French troops in 1799, contained text written in three different scripts – Egyptian hieroglyphics, Egyptian Demotic (developed from hieroglyphics) and Ancient Greek. Eventually, a translation between the three scripts was achieved in 1822, by Jean-Francois Champollion, a French scholar of ancient languages.

Discussing the photograph

▶ Explain to the class what the photograph shows (point out the lovely colours) and tell them where these hieroglyphics were found.

▶ Tell the class how hieroglyphics were not understood for many hundreds of years by English speakers. Explain how each picture (hieroglyph) represents a different sound or word.

▶ Get the children to identify particular images that they can find amongst the hieroglyphs.

▶ Discuss why they may have been written on a coffin (they are spells to ward off evil as the body travels into the afterlife).

Activities

▶ Help the children to research further information about the Book of the Dead during a whole-class ICT lesson using the Internet.

▶ Use the text 'Hieroglyphics' (photocopiable page 54) in conjunction with this photograph and give the children small word games to play with the hieroglyphs. They could find symbols to make their names.

▶ Help the children to locate the period from which the hieroglyphics on the coffin in the photograph date on the timeline (photocopiable page 53).

▶ Challenge the children to invent a picture code of their own and to make their own page of hieroglyphics. In pairs they could write messages in code to each other, providing a key to the code in order for their partner to decipher the message.

▶ Suggest the children make up spells to protect themselves, like those found in The Book of the Dead. Put these together into a modern Book of the Dead.

▶ Read the extract 'The old master scribe' (photocopiable page 56) with the children so they understand how hieroglyphics were used.

The Great Pyramids

This photograph shows the three Great Pyramids at Giza. The largest pyramid that can be seen in the photograph is referred to as the Great Pyramid and is one of the seven ancient wonders of the world. The largest of the three is known as the Great Pyramid of Khufu (or Cheops, which is the Greek version of the name) and was built first. It is 230 metres along its side and is 146 metres high. It is made from limestone blocks, which become gradually smaller at the summit. It has been estimated that there are approximately 2.6 million blocks which make up the pyramid, weighing about 7 million tonnes. The rock was cut from nearby quarries, hauled to the site and then hoisted into place. Inside the pyramid a series of steep, narrow passages lead to the burial chamber of King Khufu, of the fourth dynasty, who died about 2600BC. Leading to the burial chamber is a Grand Gallery and inside the chamber is the king's sarcophagus. There would have been a vast treasure store of all the things that belonged to the king during his life buried with him. However, this has all been taken by tomb robbers over the centuries and now only the heavy stone sarcophagus remains.

The other two pyramids were built for Khufus's dynasty. The second pyramid was built by his son, King Khafra, and the third pyramid by Menkaure, King Khafra's son.

Illustration of the pyramids

This illustration shows the Great Pyramids as if seen from above. Each pyramid has a straight causeway leading from the Nile up to it. The causeways have a temple at each end. In the middle in front of the three pyramids, sits the Sphinx, looking out over the Nile. To the left of the smallest pyramid there can be seen smaller pyramids, known as the Queens' Pyramids, so named because they are thought to have been built to house the queens of the three pharaohs buried in the Great Pyramids. There are many theories about why the pyramids were laid out as they are, but the actual reason is not known. The rectangular-shaped buildings are called mastabas, and house the remains of attendants and other family members of the pharaohs.

Discussing the pictures

▶ Look at the photograph 'The Great Pyramids' and ask the children if they know what these are, and where they are.

▶ Ask if anyone has been to Egypt and seen the pyramids.

▶ Discuss the huge size of the pyramids, noting the figures of the people on camels in the foreground of the photograph.

▶ Focus the children on the pyramids' shape and construction. Can the children suggest why the pyramids were built in this shape and what the reasons may have been? (It was a simple shape to make and it produced a very strong structure. Point out the triangular faces on a pyramid in class and discuss/demonstrate the rigidity of triangles.)

▶ Ask the children if they know why the pyramids were built, and who they were built for. Explain about the three pharaohs who built them.

▶ Look at the 'Illustration of the pyramids' and get the children to note the layout of the pyramids on the ground. Encourage them to suggest possible reasons for this layout. For example, do the children think they were deliberately built in this way, or that it was accidental?

▶ Talk about how the pyramids will have been built by many hundreds of slaves, and explain how they are made from huge blocks of stone.

▶ Ask if anyone knows what the seven ancient wonders of the world are, and if anyone can name them. Explain that the largest Great Pyramid is the only remaining wonder left.

▶ Look carefully at the 'Illustration of the pyramids' with the children and explain what the various smaller buildings around the pyramids are.

Activities

▶ Look together at the 'Map of Ancient Egypt' (provided on the CD) and locate Giza on it, explaining that this is where the Great Pyramids are.

▶ Ask the children to locate the period in which the Great Pyramid was built on the timeline on photocopiable page 53.

▶ Look at solid mathematical shapes and ask the children to identify the shape that the pyramids were built in. Get them to count the number of sides and faces of the pyramids.

▶ Provide net shapes of pyramids on thin card for the children to make their own.

▶ Set up a 'hot seat' situation, in which you take on the role of a slave who helped to build the pyramids. Challenge the children to ask you a series of questions, which could include how you coped, how the stone was moved and so on.

▶ Provide art materials of different kinds for the children to draw their own pictures of the Great Pyramids, seen either by day or by night.

The Sphinx

The Great Sphinx, situated at the foot of the pyramids at Giza, was built for King Khafra, the son of Khufu. The pyramid of Khufu can be seen in the background of this photograph. The Sphinx has the body of a lion and a human head, thought to resemble the face of Khafra. It is 20 metres high and 70 metres long, and is believed to have been carved out of a large rocky mound at the site. There are traces of red and yellow paint on its head which suggests that it was once painted in these colours. The body of the statue was once covered in desert sand, and only the head was visible. However, since the sand has been removed the figure has been deteriorating. The meaning of the word *sphinx* is uncertain, but some think it may relate to the Egyptian words meaning *living image*.

Discussing the photograph

▶ Ask the class if they have seen this picture before, and if anyone can tell you what it is called.

▶ Explain where it lies, next to the three Great Pyramids (one of which can be seen in the background).

▶ Can any of the children discern whether the head looks like a human head or an animal head? Explain to them that it has a human head with the body of a lion and that the face was meant to resemble King Khafra, who commissioned the sphinx as part of his pyramid complex.

▶ Look closely at the statue with the children and point out how it is becoming worn away by the desert winds. Discuss the use of the words *erosion* and *wind erosion*.

▶ Explain how only the head of the Sphinx was visible above the sands that had covered it at one time. Talk about how it is now being worn away since it was uncovered. Ask the children to think how it could be protected from further damage.

Activities

▶ Look at the 'Map of Ancient Egypt' (provided on the CD) with the class and locate Giza on it, explaining that this is where the Sphinx stands in the desert.

▶ Suggest the children find other mythical creatures from Ancient Egypt. Give them reference books and access to the Internet and CD-ROMs, and get them to draw their findings. Use these drawings for a class display on Ancient Egyptian mythical creatures.

▶ Use clay or Mod-Roc for the children to make their own sphinx models. Remind them how the Great Sphinx's face was carved to look like Khafra's face, and challenge them to create a sphinx for their own pyramid complex.

Ordinary Egyptian homes

Very few examples of the houses of ordinary Ancient Egyptian people have survived for archaeologists to explore. However, it is known that society was very highly organised and that people carried out many different jobs. The illustration shows how much work was carried out at home, with mothers caring for their children, people cooking and a basket weaver working under a shaded area on the roof. A water carrier and merchant can be seen in the street below, going about their work. The house itself appears to be built on two levels, from stone or mud brick, with a smaller upper storey added on top of the flat roof of the ground floor area. Much use is made of the roof space, no doubt because of the climate, and woven rush shades as well as cloths are used to enable people to relax or work out of the rays of the sun. The building is kept cool by the thick walls and few windows, and the doorways are kept open to increase the flow of cool air.

Although not evident in the illustration, some houses have been discovered with cellars. The furniture that an ordinary Egyptian family would have had in their homes would have included a few stools and low tables, a bed and some chests to store things in. The furniture would have been made plainly from wood. Pottery was used for the storage of many forms of food and drink, and it is evident that music was enjoyed at home.

Discussing the illustration

▶ Ask the children what kind of picture this is, and why they think this (it is an artist's illustration drawn in modern times).

▶ Ask the children how they think the artist knew what a house in Ancient Egyptian times would have looked like. Discuss the use of different sources of information that can be drawn upon today, such as archaeological remains, artefacts and written accounts.

▶ Ask children to identify the different parts of the houses. Explain how in some Ancient Egyptian homes there was a cellar.

▶ Ask for volunteers to point out the different jobs that they can see being carried out in the houses, and in the street.

▶ Notice the large jars against the wall of the house and discuss what these are likely to have been used for.

▶ Note the lack of large windows and discuss the reasons for this.

▶ Point out some objects that can be seen around the houses, and talk about how we know about these things today (from objects that have been found at historical excavation sites).

Activities

▶ Ask the children to draw pictures of their own houses and then to compare them with the illustration of a house from Ancient Egyptian times. Provide the children with a two-column grid, with the headings *Ancient* and *Modern* and ask them to list the features of the two houses in each column.

▶ Using another two-column grid, ask the children to list the features of their own modern house and those of the Ancient Egyptian house that are the same and those that are different. Ask them to write a sentence below the grid summarising the reasons for the differences.

▶ Ask the children, in small groups, to choose one of the jobs that they can see being carried out in the illustration, and to find out more about how it was performed in Ancient Egyptian times. Get them to write a report on their findings to present to the rest of the class. Remind them to write with their intended audience in mind.

▶ Talk about the way of life of people who lived in these houses, such as how hard they had to work, the very hot weather, and so on. Discuss the things that they might do at different times of the day, such as rest under some shade in the afternoons; going to bed early because of the dark. Set the children the task of working in pairs to write a story about a day in the life of an Ancient Egyptian child.

Temple at Luxor

This photograph shows the pylon, or monumental gateway, to the temple in modern Luxor (Thebes in Ancient Egyptian times, the capital of Egypt during the time of the New Kingdom). The construction of the vast complex of temples at Luxor was started by King Amenhotep III, who reigned between 1390 and 1353BC, and was added to over the centuries, finally being completed by Rameses II. When the temple was first built it was dedicated to the gods of Amun, Mut and Khons. The avenue leading up to the gateway is flanked by an avenue of sphinxes with rams' heads. These are set back some way from the pathway and are out of view in the photograph, but can just be seen on the right-edge. On either side of the gateway is a huge seated statue of Rameses II. In front of these there were originally two great obelisks, 25 metres high. As the photograph shows, however, only one of these remains today. The other obelisk has been removed and now stands in the Place de la Concorde in Paris.

A temple

This illustration shows a typical temple of Ancient Egypt. While many temples have survived in good condition, most ordinary buildings, such as people's homes, have disappeared. This suggests that temples were specially built to last, probably because of the importance the Egyptians attached to them. Temples were built in every community, as homes for the gods' spirits, where the pharaoh could talk to them. The pharaohs were considered equal to the gods, since they were considered to be like the gods and able to communicate with them themselves. The pharaoh was considered the high-priest of a temple and the temple's priests performed their day-to-day duties there in the pharaoh's name. Ordinary Egyptian people did not enter the temples, it was considered the realm of the priests and the pharaohs only. The temple did house its own staff, however, which would have included scribes and cooks.

In much the same way as Greek temples, those of Ancient Egypt were built to the same characteristic shape and design. Their great gateways would be flanked by obelisks and great statues of the pharaohs they had been built for. The outside of the temple would be covered with hieroglyphics and paintings, depicting and explaining important religious stories. Some temples were extended by each new pharaoh of a dynasty, adding more buildings to create a large complex over time.

Discussing the pictures

▶ Explain to the class that the photograph 'Temple at Luxor' shows the entrance to a great temple, built long ago by a number of pharaohs, including Rameses II.
▶ Discuss the location of Luxor, and explain that this is the modern name for the Ancient Egyptian city of Thebes.
▶ Discuss the size of the temple, and ask the children if they think the temple was a large one by what they can see in the photograph. Explain that it was built on a grand scale, and point out the columns that can be seen stretching back through the gateway.
▶ Ask the children to identify details in the photograph, such as the statues of Rameses II himself, the sphinx and the tall column.
▶ Does anyone know what the tall column is called? Tell the class that it is called an obelisk, and ask if they notice anything unusual about the placing of the obelisk. Ask questions to encourage the children to think about how it could have been one of a pair, like the statues of Rameses II. Tell the children where the other obelisk is now.
▶ Talk to the children about why temples were built in Egypt and about the gods they were dedicated to. Explain who the gods were that the temple at Luxor was dedicated to.
▶ Look together at the illustration 'A temple' and ask the children what they think it shows (how temples would have appeared during Ancient Egyptian times). Ask them to consider how an illustrator could have drawn this picture today (encourage them to think of how historians use artefacts and historical sites to make inferences and deductions about life in the past).
▶ Ask the children what they notice in the illustration that would not be seen as clearly at the remains of temples today (the detailed pictures and hieroglyphics, the people as they may have looked).
▶ Discuss how the temple would have been painted in bright colours and the whole scene would have been very impressive.
▶ Discuss how we know that the Egyptians used colours on temples (traces of red and yellow paint have been found on some monuments).

Activities

▶ Explain how high the obelisk in the photograph 'Temple at Luxor' is, and get the children to try to estimate this height. Ask them to compare it with a building they can see, or that they have visited. They could draw the obelisk and the building they are comparing it to, marking the height of each on their drawing.
▶ Provide modelling materials for the children to create their own obelisks and statues, based on those in the pictures.
▶ Give the children a copy of the 'Map of Ancient Egypt' (provided on the CD) and ask them to locate Luxor on it (Thebes).
▶ Create a large wall painting or collage of a temple and get the children to paint hieroglyphs and designs from their knowledge of Ancient Egypt onto it. They could make a 3-D image, with obelisks and statues standing in front of their temple.
▶ Ask the children to find out about the gods of Amun, Mut and Khons, using the Internet.

Rameses II and Abu Simbel

Abu Simbel, far from the coast and in a less accessible place, was for a long time the least known to travellers of the historic Ancient Egyptian sites. Built by Rameses II between 1279 and 1212BC, the temple was created out of a sandstone cliff. The temple's entrance is flanked by colossal statues of Rameses himself, seated. This photograph shows a detail of two of them. These giant statues, over 20 metres high, testify to the fact that Rameses II was thought by the Ancient Egyptians themselves to be a great pharaoh, partly because of his victories in foreign wars. The statues appear to be in reasonable condition, almost as they would have been in the ancient past. There are cartouches on the arms and body of the statues, probably describing the identity of Rameses.

Inside the entrance to the temple, there are eight pillars carved to represent Rameses II as the god Osiris, the ruler of the dead. The columns also help to support the construction of the temple. The walls inside the temple are covered in hieroglyphics which tell of the victories that Rameses had enjoyed in wars.

Rameses II and the temple at Karnak

Another colossal statue of Rameses II, one of many that were made for him, is shown in this photograph. The statue has been restored and stands before a pylon (gateway) of the great temple of Amun in Karnak. The temple is so named because Rameses dedicated the building of the main temple at this site to the god Amun, and this is famous as the largest columned room in the world. Located to the north of Luxor, the construction of the temple took place over a long period, beginning before the Middle Kingdom (around 2000BC) and being completed in the New Kingdom, about 1600 years later. The temple at Luxor was connected with the temple at Karnak by a great avenue of ram-headed sphinxes. This was completed during the New Kingdom, by Rameses.

Rameses II reigned between 1279 and 1212BC. He reigned for 67 years and is one of the most famous of the Egyptian pharaohs, also known as Rameses the Great, partly because he built many monuments, including those at Abu Simbel, and partly because he led many successful war campaigns during his reign. He had many wives and concubines, and is thought to have fathered over 100 children. Between the feet of the statue of Rameses in the photograph is a smaller statue, thought to be one of his daughters, Princess Bentanta. His favourite wife was Nefertari, and her tomb is said to be the most beautiful in the Valley of the Queens.

Discussing the photographs
▶ Look with the children at the two photographs showing statues of Rameses II and ask if they can guess what type of person would have had these statues made.
▶ Tell them that the statues were made to resemble Rameses II, who was considered to be a great pharaoh.
▶ Discuss with the class why Rameses II felt he needed these colossal statues of himself made. Explain how he also had his name and reports about his life inscribed inside buildings.
▶ Explain that the statues in the photographs stand outside the temples at Abu Simbel and Karnak, and tell the children about each of these constructions.
▶ Talk about how one of the things Rameses II is known for is his great building works, which included the temples at Karnak and Abu Simbel, shown in the photographs.
▶ Ask the children to imagine what the effect of these enormous statues would have had on ordinary people who lived at the time (they might have been fearful or in awe of them, and of Rameses himself).
▶ Ask the children to think about how the temples in the photographs were made, by whom, and how much they would have cost. Get them to think about who had to do the work and who had to pay for them.
▶ Discuss whether today we would think that building great temples such as the one at Karnak would be the right thing for a king or queen to do.

Activities
▶ Help the children to locate the period of Rameses II on the timeline on photocopiable page 53.
▶ Give the children a copy of the 'Map of Ancient Egypt' (provided on the CD) and ask them to find both Karnak and Abu Simbel on it. Ask what they notice about the two locations (Karnak is closely connected to other important Egyptian sites, such as the Valley of the Kings and Thebes, whilst Abu Simbel is in a more remote location).
▶ Give the children a copy of the photograph 'Temple at Luxor' and explain how this temple was built after the temple at Karnak and connected to it.
▶ Set the children the task of carrying out further research into the history and life of Rameses II, his dynasty and his family. They could find out about his wives, in particular, Queen Nefertari. Ask them to make notes which they can use to give short talks to the rest of the class on their findings after they have completed their research.
▶ Challenge the children to write an imaginative account of a procession, headed by the Rameses II, going along the avenue into either of the temples at Luxor or Karnak.

NOTES ON THE PHOTOCOPIABLE PAGES

Word and sentence cards
PAGES 49–52

The word and sentence cards include a number of specific types of vocabulary:
▶ words associated with the passing of time, such as *ancient, modern, BC, AD*
▶ words associated with Ancient Egypt, such as *Nile, pharaoh, sphinx*
▶ words associated with life after death, such as *god, tomb, mummy.*

Encourage the children to think of other appropriate words to build up a word bank for the topic of Ancient Egypt. The sentence cards suggest ways of using the key words to summarise knowledge about the period and the children could be encouraged to use all the words in the same way.

Activities
▶ Give the children sets of word cards to use in their own writing on Ancient Egypt.
▶ Give the children a number of the word cards, randomly ordered, and ask them to group the words according to themes, such as *mummy* and *sarcophagus* in a 'life after death' group.
▶ Play 20 questions and 'hangman' games based on the key words.

Timeline of Ancient Egypt
PAGE 53

This timeline can be used to introduce children to the notion of chronology over a substantial period of time. Children can begin to understand how timelines need to be flexible and drawn to different scales, in just the same way as maps, and that the scale and size of a timeline will vary depending on the information it needs to contain. This timeline is useful as an overview of a long period and gives only the major events and spans.

This timeline can be usefully used alongside the pictures on the Ancient Egypt Resource Gallery on the CD. It could be adapted for the classroom in the form of a wall frieze, or represented as a long string stretched along one wall with pictures from the period hung from it, including the children's own pictures as the topic progresses. The kind of timeline shown here can also be useful at the end of the topic, for checking the children's success in grasping ideas of sequence, chronology and, for those at that stage, understanding of the use of dates and the terms *BC* and *AD*. Assessment like this could be carried out by asking the children to create their own version of the timeline, or by giving them a blank, or partially completed, outline to complete with the events in the correct order, placing pictures in the appropriate places.

Discussing the timeline
▶ Ask the class at the beginning of the topic what they think this timeline shows and if they know any of the information on it.
▶ Clarify with the children what the dates on the timeline mean. Discuss how this timeline is quite small, yet it still represents many thousands of years. Ensure that the children understand how it does this.
▶ Look together at the 'reading direction' of the timeline. Explain that this represents the passing of time and main events that happened during that time, and that it needs to be read from top to bottom.
▶ Talk about key events, personalities and periods during the time of the Ancient Egyptians, working along the timeline, and add more information as appropriate as the topic progresses.

Activities
▶ Make a class timeline, using the timeline on photocopiable page 53 as an example. Ask the children to add any other pictures or photographs of things related to Ancient Egypt that they have found in appropriate places on the class timeline.
▶ Suggest the children find other timelines of Ancient Egypt in the class collection of books, and that they use these to develop and add to either the class timeline, or their own copy of the timeline. They could also add further details after reading stories and accounts of Ancient Egyptian life, such as those on photocopiable pages 54 and 56.
▶ Give the children an almost blank timeline of Ancient Egypt with only a few key dates included and ask them to complete it. This will provide useful assessment evidence.

Hieroglyphics

PAGE 54

This information text gives children a simple account of what hieroglyphics were. It explains how long ago they began to be used and how for a time their meaning was lost and then rediscovered. The uses of hieroglyphics is explained and some simple guidance on how to read them is included. The children can use the examples of hieroglyphics in different ways: to decipher meanings; to recreate; as a stimulus for artwork.

Discussing the text

► Read through the text with the children and study the examples of hieroglyphics.

► Ask the children to tell you what hieroglyphics were used for.

► Discuss, while looking at the examples, how they were read in several different directions.

► Talk about how they represented different things, and find volunteers to explain what they represented. For example, a single sound, syllables, or whole words. Explain how some symbols were included as guides for the reader, so their significance in the text was totally different.

► Discuss how hard it must have been to understand all these different features of the script and for historians to decipher what texts said.

► Ask the children to explain the meaning of the word *cartouche*.

Activities

► Help the children to locate the approximate time when hieroglyphics are thought to have been first used on the class timeline.

► Ask the children to write their names using hieroglyphics. They could make this up, drawing upon the examples on the photocopiable sheet or creating their own, or they could look up what the different symbols represent on the Internet.

► Organise the children to work in groups to discuss ways of creating cartouches for their own names. Provide materials for them to draw their own cartouches.

Howard Carter's discoveries

PAGE 55

This text could be read by individuals or groups of more able readers. It gives a brief account of the adventures of the archaeologist Howard Carter and the discoveries he made in the Valley of the Kings. It will be a useful text to read alongside the images on the CD of 'The Valley of the Kings', 'Tomb of Tutankhamun' and 'Funeral mask of Tutankhamun'. It is a text that could be used to stimulate children to carry out further research into the details of the discoveries and to read more about the 'curse of the mummy', from which it was thought Lord Carnarvon died soon after opening the tomb.

Discussing the text

► Read through the text with the whole class or, alternatively, give copies to more able readers to use in small groups or independently.

► Discuss with the children the period in which Howard Carter was born (Victorian), and help them to understand the dates used in the extract.

► Explain how it was that two English people were permitted to carry out excavations in an Egyptian site. Point out that at the time when permission was granted to Lord Carnarvon, Egypt was a British Protectorate, and the Egyptian government may not have had much choice in the matter.

► Discuss the excitement that Carter and his archaeologists must have felt when the steps were found in the rubble in the Valley of the Kings.

► Talk about the progress of the archaeologists from one part of the tomb to the next, and how frustrating it must have been to keep coming to sealed doorways.

► Ask the children to think of reasons why this tomb had not been emptied of all its possessions before, pointing out how it had been opened before but resealed again. Discuss

Photograph © Nova Developments

why this may have been (fear of the spells of the Ancient Egyptians, reverence and respect for the tomb). Discuss how it was a much smaller tomb than the others that had previously been robbed, and how the tomb robbers might not have been able to find it.

▶ Talk about how he must have felt when Carter opened the final doorway to see the shrine itself.

Activities

▶ Help the children to locate the Valley of the Kings on the 'Map of Ancient Egypt' (provided on the CD).

▶ Ask the class to put together a bank of words describing the feelings of the archaeologists when they found the treasures. The children can then use their word bank to assist them in writing an imaginative description of the event.

▶ Challenge more able children to use the account and their own research to create a timeline of the life of Howard Carter.

The old master scribe

PAGE 56

This brief extract gives some idea of what was involved in learning to become a scribe. Clearly, the old master scribe is trying to teach the boy to learn to write well so he can take up the role of scribe himself later in life. The extract highlights the training involved in becoming a scribe – learning to write the script of the land and practising hard each day. The Ancient Egyptians must have placed great value upon their books and writing, since these lasted longer than they themselves. There is certainly honour bound up in the old master scribe's telling of what it is to be a scribe.

Discussing the extract

▶ Read through the extract with the children, helping them to understand the language used in it.

▶ Discuss what the term *scribe* means.

▶ Ask the children to recall the training involved to become a scribe.

▶ Ask if they can think of any disadvantages of being a scribe (being shut inside to work, having to write and copy all the time).

▶ Can the children find clues that tell them being a scribe is hard work (*...paused and wiped his brow, practising his signs for hours every day*).

▶ Ask volunteers to find phrases that indicate the honour surrounding the role of scribe in the text (*...the power and knowledge of writing, ...the mysteries of the land*).

Activities

▶ Ask the children to make a poster advertising the job of a scribe. As part of the poster, they will need to list the benefits of the job and illustrate it with the tools of the trade and with hieroglyphics.

▶ Challenge the children to research further information about being a scribe. Get them to list the types of writing that would have needed to be done as a scribe, such as listing the king's purchases and making orders, writing Books of the Dead.

Glossary

PAGE 57

This writing frame is designed for more able readers to work with in order to build up their own glossary of Ancient Egyptian terms. It is not necessarily an inclusive list of words, and very able children could be encouraged to build on it to create a more comprehensive collection of words. Once completed, it could be used by less able readers and writers to help them in their own independent work.

The passing of time word cards

ancient

modern

today

BC

AD

Ancient Egypt developed thousands of years before the birth of Christ (BC).

Ancient Egypt word cards

Nile

pharaoh

sphinx

hieroglyphics

papyrus

The pharaohs built their towns, temples and pyramids along the course of the River Nile.

📖 SCHOLASTIC
PHOTOCOPIABLE

Life after death word cards (1)

god

goddess

afterlife

tomb

pyramid

mummy

mummified

sarcophagus

Book of the Dead

Ancient Egyptians believed that a dead pharaoh's body should be mummified and placed in a sealed tomb.

Timeline of Ancient Egypt

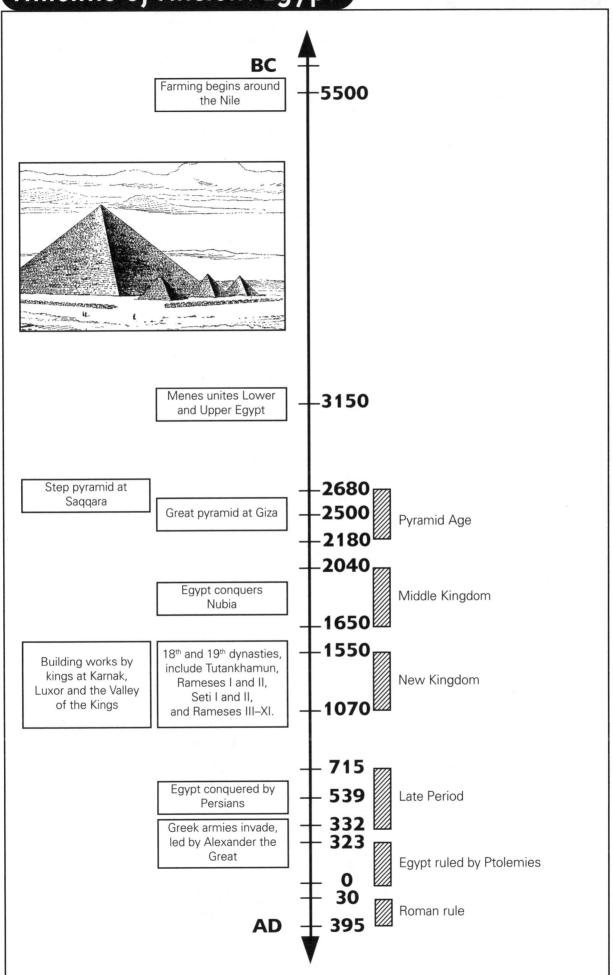

BC

Farming begins around the Nile — **5500**

Menes unites Lower and Upper Egypt — **3150**

Step pyramid at Saqqara

Great pyramid at Giza

2680
2500 Pyramid Age
2180

2040
Egypt conquers Nubia
1650 Middle Kingdom

1550
Building works by kings at Karnak, Luxor and the Valley of the Kings

18th and 19th dynasties, include Tutankhamun, Rameses I and II, Seti I and II, and Rameses III–XI.

New Kingdom
1070

715
Egypt conquered by Persians
539 Late Period

Greek armies invade, led by Alexander the Great
332
323

Egypt ruled by Ptolemies

0
30 Roman rule

AD **395**

Hieroglyphics

The Ancient Egyptians developed a script 5000 years ago, which we now know as hieroglyphics. Although hieroglyphics had been used for about 4000 years, following the end of the Egyptian empire they were lost and forgotten for 1500 years because no one could translate them. Today, thanks to the work of Jean-Francois Champollion in the 19th century, we can read the script and learn about the way of life of the Ancient Egyptians from the writing they left behind.

The Ancient Egyptians had invented a form of writing and also a written number system. The carefully drawn symbols were used either by priests or for decorating the walls of temples and sacred objects. However, a much simpler kind of writing was used for everyday writing, in which the symbols were reduced to very simple abstract shapes.

Hieroglyphs can be written in either rows or columns and can be read from either left or right. This is one of the features that made translation impossible for so many years. A clue to the direction in which to read them is that the symbols face towards the beginning of the line. There were different kinds of hieroglyphics. Some hieroglyphs represented one single sound, just like the letters of the Roman alphabet which we use in writing today. Some hieroglyphs represented syllables, some whole words and others were pictures of objects to help the reader.

Hieroglyphics were also written inside cartouches (oval shapes). When they were written like this, they represented the names of the pharaohs.

Some examples of hieroglyphics are shown below:

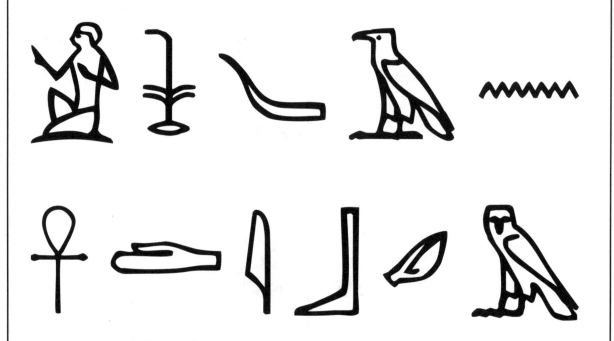

◣ SCHOLASTIC
PHOTOCOPIABLE

Howard Carter's discoveries

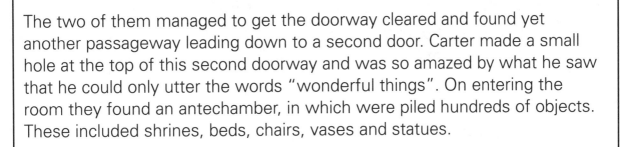

In the early 19th century the English archaeologist Howard Carter joined forces with Lord Carnarvon, who had a special concession from the Egyptian government to excavate the Valley of the Kings. Carter felt sure that the tomb of Tutankhamun was somewhere in the Valley of the Kings.

On 4 November 1922 archaeologists working with Carter found some steps amongst the rubble in a pyramid leading down to a blocked doorway. Peering through a hole at the top of the door Carter found that the space behind it was full of more rubble, but the plaster which blocked the entrance had seals on it, suggesting that the doorway was an important one. Carter wrote to Lord Carnarvon to set out for Egypt at once.

The two of them managed to get the doorway cleared and found yet another passageway leading down to a second door. Carter made a small hole at the top of this second doorway and was so amazed by what he saw that he could only utter the words "wonderful things". On entering the room they found an antechamber, in which were piled hundreds of objects. These included shrines, beds, chairs, vases and statues.

Yet another door, sealed with plaster, led into the burial chamber itself, where even greater treasures were revealed. The whole of the chamber was filled with the golden shrine of Tutankhamun. When the shrine was opened, four more shrines were found inside it, one inside the other. The very last one held the coffin, inside which was found the mummy of Tutankhamun himself, along with his now famous death mask.

Carter and Carnarvon called for a large team of experts to help photograph all the things they had found before they were removed. They were

preserved and carefully packed so that they could be safely transported to Cairo, where they are now kept in the Egyptian Museum. It took ten years for all of this work to be completed.

Soon after the tomb was opened, however, Lord Carnarvon became ill from an infected mosquito bite and died. For many years, the death of anyone involved in the excavation of the tomb was said to be the result of the "curse of the mummy".

The old master scribe

The old master scribe paused and wiped his brow. "As a scribe you are given the power and knowledge of writing. First, you must learn the common script of the land so you can perform everyday tasks. After that, if you are lucky and talented, you will also learn the sacred script. Those who learn the sacred script will learn the secrets of the gods and the mysteries of the land."

The old master scribe reached behind him and brought out a small wooden palette. He held it out to the boy. "This is for you. Once you have learned to read and write, you will have many opportunities in the world. Practise your signs well and you will go far." Then, he stood up.

The boy said goodbye to the old master scribe and left his home. For many years he studied to be a scribe, practising his signs for hours every day. It was difficult work, and sometimes he hated school. But he worked hard.

Finally, he was ready to leave scribe school. He had done well and was offered a position as a priest in a temple.

Long after the old master scribe had died, the young man still thought about their meeting. He never forgot what the old man had taught him about the importance of learning the scripts, and the honour of being a scribe.

SCHOLASTIC
PHOTOCOPIABLE

Glossary

▷ Create your own glossary. Notice how the words in the glossary are in alphabetical order. Use the example that has been done for you as a starting point.

afterlife	The life a pharaoh was believed to have led after he had died.
antechamber	
archaeologist	
canopic jars	
death mask	
hieroglyphics	
mummy	
Nile	
papyrus	
pharaoh	
pyramid	
sarcophagus	
scribe	
shabti	
sphinx	
temple	
tomb	

LOCAL HISTORY

Content, skills and concepts

This chapter relates to Unit 18 of the QCA Scheme of Work for history at Key Stage 2, 'What was it like to live here in the past?'. It is assumed that this unit will be taught mainly to Years 3 or 4, but it can also be adapted for teaching to children in older age groups.

Recounting stories about the past, and looking for similarities and differences between the past and the present, are prior learning activities which will have introduced relevant skills and concepts to the children before they progress to the skills and concepts in this unit of work. This chapter includes suggestions for the extension of these and other skills, such as recognising change and continuity, and the ability to select and use information to support a discussion, for example about the reasons for changes in a local area. Investigating change within the locality, and also the reasons for those changes, are the focus of this chapter.

Resources on the CD-ROM

The Local history Resource Gallery on the CD-ROM provides both contemporary and modern photographs, maps and extracts from documents. Teacher's notes containing background information about these resources are provided in this chapter, along with ideas for further work involving them.

Photocopiable pages

Photocopiable resources are also provided within the book and in PDF format on the CD-ROM, from which they can be printed out. These include:

▶ word and sentence cards highlighting the essential vocabulary of this topic
▶ an extract from the Domesday Book
▶ a 'census form' for the children to complete
▶ a research checklist
▶ an interviewing frame.

Teacher's notes accompany all the photocopiable text resources in this chapter. They include suggestions for developing discussion about the sheets and for ways of using them for whole class, group or individual activities. More able readers and writers will be able to read and use the writing frames independently, but some children will need help in interpreting and using them. It may be helpful to pair a good reader with a less able reader when using these resources.

History skills

Skills such as observing, describing, using time-related vocabulary, sequencing, understanding the meaning of dates, comparing, inferring, listening, speaking, reading and writing are involved in the activities in this chapter. For example, there is great opportunity for the children to develop descriptive vocabulary when describing the resources included on the CD.

Historical understanding

This chapter provides an overarching aim for children to begin to develop a more detailed knowledge of the past and their ability to sequence and date events independently, through their understanding of the context and content of the factual information they use. They will begin to give reasons for events and use other sources to find further information. They will also have the opportunity to extend their skills in using descriptive language and specific time-related terms when discussing resources. Communication skills of various types are encouraged throughout this chapter.

Photograph © Photodisc, Inc.

NOTES ON THE CD-ROM RESOURCES

A Victorian census

This image shows a page from an enumerator's book, in which the details needed for the census were noted down by hand. The enumerator would call at each household and talk to the occupants to find out the information required. This extract is taken from the 1901 census of Royal Leamington Spa, in Warwickshire. Such information is very revealing if used in conjunction with a walk around a local area which has houses and other buildings dating from Victorian times, or when used with photographs of these buildings. The census can add considerably to the children's knowledge and understanding of the area. It can help them in confirming the date and period of the buildings they have seen, and in providing more detailed information about who would have lived in them, their social status, the size of their families, where they were born and what kind of jobs they did. Other subtle changes can be picked up from census data, such as the choice of Christian names then – commonly used names have now changed a great deal since Victorian times (although some are now coming back into popular use, such as Elizabeth, Amy, Hannah and Sarah). In certain areas, census data of this kind can reveal population changes and immigration trends, showing where people came from and when they settled in the country. Street and trade directories and, of course, oral history records are all similarly useful resources and can be used in conjunction with census data, where available.

Discussing the census
▶ Look at the census closely with the class. Discuss how it was made and who would have written down the information.
▶ Discuss whether it is easy to read or not, and why this is.
▶ Look at the style of handwriting and explain to the children that this would have been done by a person called an 'enumerator', who had the job of going round and finding out who lived in each house.
▶ Talk about why the census was, and still is, made every ten years (to keep a record of the population and to know how it is changing, and to know how much can be raised in taxes).
▶ Look at the type of information the census shows, such as where people were born, the work they did and the people in their families.
▶ Discuss why people would want to know this sort of information. Compare these reasons with the drawing up of the Domesday Book, and discuss why this was made.

Activities
▶ Help the children to understand how long ago this census was compiled. Use the word cards on photocopiable page 74 to help the children, using words such as *decade* and *century* with them.
▶ Use the 'Census form' (photocopiable page 78) to reinforce the children's understanding of what information is included in a census and what it can be used for.
▶ Ask the children to find the place that the census deals with on a map of Britain.
▶ Ask the children to find certain specific pieces of information to ensure that they can understand how to interpret the chart form that the census data is presented in. For example, ask the children to give the name of the merchant shown on the census, or to say how many people there were in his family.
▶ Use the 'Extract from the Domesday book' (photocopiable page 77) and compare the sort of information recorded here with the census details.
▶ Get the children to design a census chart of their own, showing the kind of data that would be entered for their house, or for the house of a famous person that they admire.

A street in 1900

The houses in this photograph are the same as those listed in 'A Victorian census' (provided on the CD). They are late Victorian terraces, which would have been inhabited by people with a fairly modest income. Built in a period when there was a growing concern about public health and amenities, and about the quality of housing for the working classes, these homes have light, airy bay windows, and a small enclosed area at the front. The upstairs windows are also substantial sash windows, designed to allow as much light and fresh air into the rooms as possible. They are sturdily built in typical red brick, with slate roofs. A characteristic feature of homes in this period is the large chimney and tall chimney pots, designed to lift the smoke from coal fires away from the streets. There was concern that people should be comfortable and warm in their homes, but not a great deal of effort was made to conserve energy and heat by insulating the houses well.

A modern street

This is a photograph of the same street as shown in 'A street in 1900', but taken in modern times. In some essential aspects, the street remains the same. The houses are still there as they were originally built – both the terraces and the larger semi-detached houses at the far end of the street. In many ways the houses themselves look the same, although some small details have been changed, such as the painted brickwork in the archways of some of the houses. The road is still wide and the trees and bushes, just visible on the left of the early picture, may have grown into the larger trees that appear in the modern photograph. The neat, uniform railings in front of each house have now largely disappeared to be replaced with low brick walls in some cases and brick-built gateposts. The most obvious change, of course, is the traffic – parked cars line most of the street on both sides in the modern picture.

Discussing the photographs

▶ Show the children both pictures together. Discuss what kind of pictures they are (photographs), comparing the type of photography in each.
▶ Find volunteers to make some comparisons between the two and to note some changes, such as the cars in the modern picture.
▶ Find further individuals who will point out more subtle details of what has changed, such as the railings.
▶ Choose some children and ask them to point out all the details that have stayed the same.
▶ Discuss the reasons why some things have changed and others have stayed the same.
▶ Get the children to imagine what may or may not have changed inside the houses. For example, there will still be kitchens, living rooms and bedrooms in the modern house, but there will be different equipment in each room, such as electrical equipment in the kitchen instead of a range heated with coal.

Activities

▶ Use the word cards on photocopiable pages 75–6 to discuss the features of the two houses with the children, pointing out features such as *sash window*, *arch*, *architecture*.
▶ Take a walk around the locality of the school. Choose a street where there are Victorian houses and take a photograph of them. Ask the children to compare this photograph with the photograph of 'A street in 1900' and to list any features that they can see that are the same (such as chimney pots, railings).
▶ Use the two pictures from the CD to encourage the children to make inferences about the lives of the people who lived in these houses in the past. For example, they would mostly have walked to work or to school. Then encourage the children to make inferences about the lives of the people who live in the same houses today. For example, they may travel to work or to school by car.
▶ Challenge the children to write a time-travel adventure story based on the experiences of a child who goes back to the early 1900s and finds themselves in the same house, but in a different age.

Maps of Lancashire in 1847, 1909 and 1949

These three maps are very useful in showing change and development in the same small area over a long period of time. In the 1847 map, there is little evidence of buildings. The area seems to be made up mostly of farm land, divided into small fields, with lanes and hedges. Cowling Lane is one of the most prominent lanes running through the area. Two works, Cowling Bridge Print Works and Bleaching Works can be seen, along with an inn over on the left-hand side of the map. It might be concluded that apart from the bleaching works and fabric printing, the main occupations in the area would probably have been associated with farming.

By 1909, several things have changed. While the earlier roadways are still evident, Cowling

Lane has become Cowling Brow. Several new streets have appeared, along with more buildings, two churches and houses. There is also a new footpath (labelled F.P. at the bottom of the map). The two works are still in evidence, but their uses have changed, with one becoming a brick works and the other a cotton mill. The sandstone works shown on the 1847 map has disappeared.

By 1949, there has been considerable building in the area. Most of the open fields have been replaced with streets and houses, a second mill has sprung up (Crosse Hall Mill) and the brick works seen on the 1909 map has been replaced by a concrete factory. The change in the use of this factory is perhaps one of the most significant features of the maps. It reflects the changes that were taking place in the economy and the needs of local society at the different times. By 1949 there are so many people living in the area, and so little open land, that a recreation area has had to be created along with allotment gardens. The constant feature is still the main roadway, Cowling Brow.

Discussing the maps
▶ Show the children the three maps and ask for their immediate reactions. What do they notice? (The maps all show the same place.)
▶ Explain the date of each map to the children and how they form a sequence over a period of time.
▶ Talk about how open fields are shown, how buildings are represented and what the abbreviations stand for, such as *Ch* for church, *F.P.* for footpath.
▶ Discuss what seems to have changed the most over the three periods. For example, there are mostly fields on the 1847 map, while there are a lot more houses on much of the same land on the 1949 map.
▶ Ask the children what they think has happened to the Inn, just discernible on the 1847 map.
▶ Look at the 1909 map, and ask what new buildings have appeared that were not in the area in 1847 (the two churches, houses). Talk about how church building was very widespread in the late Victorian period.
▶ Look at the 1847 map and ask the children what kind of work took place in the area. Discuss how these works changed in 1909 and again in 1949. Can anyone suggest why they might have changed?
▶ Ask the children to identify new features that appear on the 1949 map that are not there on the two earlier maps (Cowling Concrete, a recreation ground, allotment gardens).
▶ Discuss with the children the value of maps for showing historical changes and developments in local areas.

Activities
▶ Use the word cards on photocopiable page 75 when discussing the maps to reinforce the different features found on them, such as *mill* and *factory*.
▶ Use a map site on the Internet, such as www.mapzone.co.uk, to find modern and historical maps of the locality of the school, or another local area of interest that is known to the children. Print these off and make copies for the children to use in small groups. Ask the groups to make notes on the developments they can discover from their maps. Then ask the groups to report their findings to the rest of the class.
▶ Encourage the children to use the 'Research checklist' (photocopiable page 79) in conjunction with the maps they found on the Internet, and also with those provided on the CD.

A shopping street in 1905

This photograph shows one of the main shopping streets in Leamington Spa as it appeared circa 1905. Perhaps the most striking feature for us today is how bare and empty the street looks. There are no traffic signs, or cars and buses, making the whole scene appear very different from the present day. In many other respects the street is as one would expect. There is a main road, pavements and street lighting (although the street lamps are different from modern day lamp-posts) and the shops look neat and tidy. Although colour is not apparent because of the black and white photography of the time, the names above the shops seem to be quite discreetly written. The whole scene is one of tranquillity and calm due to the lack of people and traffic.

A modern shopping street

This is a modern photograph of the main shopping street in Leamington Spa, taken in 2002. While the buildings themselves appear very similar to those in the 'A shopping street in 1905' photograph, the shops and the street itself have changed considerably in their appearance. Traffic signs are prominent so as to be clearly visible for passing drivers, and the road itself has bold traffic markings on it. Cars are coming and going in all directions. They almost fill the road outside the shops, along with queuing buses. The street is gaily decorated with plants and flowers, and the road itself looks extremely busy, with people going about their daily business. The whole scene is one of business. An aspect of many large towns and cities is congestion, which has now begun to be addressed through the imposition of quite high charges to deter people from driving in urban centres. One other main change is that the church at the top of the street has gone, replaced with a grassy area, of which the trees can be seen here.

Discussing the photographs
▶ Look at both of the photographs at the same time with the class, and ask them to order them chronologically.
▶ See if the children can locate each picture roughly in time.
▶ Find individuals who can identify the characteristic features of each photograph.
▶ Choose volunteers to point out the things they can see that have changed and the things that have stayed the same.
▶ Review the changes with the class and point out how these can be categorised, for example into aspects such as traffic, or display and advertising.
▶ Talk together about the reasons for the changes that have been identified.
▶ Ask the children which street they would prefer to do their shopping in and why.

Activities
▶ Set the children the task of writing a fictional paragraph about each picture from the point of view of a child going shopping with a grandparent.
▶ Divide the class into two. Put one half into the role of people in favour of driving to the shops in their cars, while the others have to take the stance of those who want to get rid of cars in urban areas. Suggest they discuss their ideas in small groups and write down the points of their arguments, then get together and pool all their arguments. Set up a class debate about the issue and introduce this with a brief account of the congestion charges that have been introduced for drivers entering the centre of London at certain times of the day. Finally, hold a vote to see what the majority opinion is on the issue.
▶ Provide musical instruments for the children to recreate the sounds they would hear in both the 1905 street and in the 21st-century street.
▶ Provide the children with extracts from street directories and/or trade directories for your local shopping area. Ask them to use these to compare the shops and buildings in the past with those in the present day. They can research the sort of shops found in the locality in the past by using the Internet, local reference books or by asking any family who live locally.

Amy Mews

This unusual building is an interesting example of how the use of a building can change over time. It was originally built as a school, St Mary's Radford Road School, in Leamington Spa, Warwickshire, in 1858. Inside, there was one large room and a smaller room for infants, with a playground attached. It was built in a gothic style. Its windows were diamond paned and built in tall arches. The building is now a private house. It has retained many of its features, such as the gothic windows, the buttresses, gables and arched doorway on the left of the photograph. Modern additions are visible in the photograph, such as the plaque on the end wall and the small windows that have been let into the roof at intervals. While the changes

inside the house are likely to have been fairly substantial it remains relatively unchanged from the time when the exterior was built.

Discussing the photograph

▶ Look at the photograph with the children and discuss what type of building they can see. Ask the children to share their ideas and to give reasons for their opinions.

▶ Focus on the details of the building, such as the windows, brickwork, design, doorway, and talk about how these details show that the building is an old one. For example, the panes of glass in the windows.

▶ Tell the children that this is now a private house, but was once a school. Ask if they can identify any parts of the house that might be the same since the building changed its use, such as the shape of the windows and the doorway.

▶ Ask the children why they think it is no longer used as a school. Explain how it is probably too small now as the area around it has probably developed and there are too many children to attend such a small school.

▶ Discuss how the use of buildings change over time and ask if the children can identify any modern features that have been added to Amy Mews in modern times.

Activities

▶ Use the word cards on photocopiable page 76 to help explain the architectural features to the children, such as *gable* and *arch*.

▶ Provide drawing materials and challenge the children to draw the interior of Amy Mews showing what rooms it might contain. They could draw pictures as a cross section or, if they have previously learned about plans, as a plan of the ground floor.

▶ Ask the children to write an imaginary account of spending a day at Amy Mews when it was a school. They will need to consider whether it had a playground, how many children would have been present, how many teachers, and so on.

Aerial picture of Warwick

This is an aerial photograph of the town of Warwick in the present day. The picture is very wide ranging and shows not only the centre of the city, but all the suburban areas too. The River Avon appears as a thick, dark line snaking across the length of the right-hand side of the picture. Just on the north side of the river, near the centre at the bottom of the photograph, you can make out Warwick castle. This appears as a rectangular clearing. Just to the right of the castle, some large light-coloured areas show the roofs of the boathouses belonging to Warwick Boat Club. Again, just across the road and to the right of the boat club can be seen St Nicholas Park, almost pentagonal in shape, and very neatly designed. The larger park to the north of St Nicholas Park is Priory Park. To the left of Warwick Castle, you can make out the large irregular shape of the racecourse. The town centre is just to the north of the castle and this appears as the most densely built-up part of the city. An interesting feature of the development of many towns and cities, which appears clearly on this photograph, is the way the area has developed in a series of almost concentric circles, delineated by the river and the roads. Each stage of new development and building has added another layer around the existing built-up part of the city. A modern boundary that can be seen is the road running around the western edge of the city.

Discussing the photograph

▶ Look at the map with the class and ask them to identify the built-up areas and the fields.

▶ Look at the other large green areas on the map and ask the class what they think these may be. Explain that they are parks.

▶ One large green area is not a park and has an unusual shape. Can anyone guess what this is? (The track is just visible around the edge.) Explain that it is a racecourse.

▶ Ask what other features the map shows, for example roads, the river.

▶ Point out the location of the castle and ask the children to think of reasons why it was built in this particular place (because defenders could see anyone approaching on the river).

▶ Ask the children where they think the oldest part of the town is (near the castle). Can they think why it would be near the castle?

▶ Ask the children whether they think this looks like a large town or not and ask them to give reasons for their answers.

Activities

▶ Look at the map with the class and ask them to identify north on it. Check that they know the other points of the compass and can apply these when looking at the map.

▶ Help the children to locate Warwick on a map of Britain.

▶ If possible, organise a visit to Warwick castle and/or get the children to carry out research on it, finding out when it was built, who lived in it, and so on.

▶ Give the children a copy of the 'Extract from the Domesday Book' (photocopiable page 77). Explain that this outlines details of Warwick, such as land ownership, in 1086. Ask if they can suggest the changes that have taken place in Warwick between then and now. For example, Warwick is more heavily populated now, a lot of construction has taken place.

Roman road in the past

This modern illustration shows part of a Roman road as it may have appeared in Roman times. It shows all the characteristic features of Roman roads – their straightness, regardless of the terrain; the regular rectangular blocks that they were paved with; their width and evenness. Here, we see a section near a crossroad where a Roman villa is situated. The crossroad is marked with a statue and in the foreground a milestone is visible, giving the distance to the next place of significance. The centurion, cohort of soldiers and their supplies indicate the purpose for which the road was constructed and help to explain why the Romans built their roads so straight. A native Celt is seen in the distance looking back at the Roman troops in some disquiet.

Roman road in modern times

In this illustration, the Roman road is shown as it would appear in the present day. The only feature that remains to suggest that it was originally a Roman road is its straightness. The villa has long since gone, now replaced by farmland. In the distance a town with high-rise flats can be seen. The crossroad is still there, but instead of Roman legionaries and Celts there are cars and lorries.

In place of the milestone there is a modern road sign and the Roman woman and child have been replaced by a walker reading a map. A garage stands on one corner and there is an indication of more buildings going off into the distance on the opposite side of the road. The road itself has changed in appearance, now smoothly tarmacked, with drains to keep the road clear during wet weather. The road is also marked with lines to guide the traffic. Children will be able to see these clear changes and will need to be taken beyond them to question why and how the changes have taken place.

Discussing the illustrations

▶ Look at both the illustrations at the same time with the class, and ask them to identify the periods in time that they show.

▶ Ask the children to say which picture is set in an earlier time and to explain how they know this.

▶ Ask the children to look closely at the 'Roman road in the past' illustration and to note each feature that tells them it is Roman. For example, the soldiers, the Latin writing and Roman numerals, the woman and child and the way they are dressed, the style of the villa.

▶ Ask the children to note all the details in the 'Roman road in modern times' illustration that show it is set in the present day. For example, the lorry, the cars, the modern road signs.

▶ Get the children to compare the details in the Roman illustration with those in the modern one. Talk about how we know it is a Roman road, even though it contains modern-day people and things.

▶ Ask the children why they think the changes to the Roman road have taken place.

Activities

▶ Write up on the board a list of the main changes that have taken place to the Roman road as shown in the illustrations, and get the children to suggest categories to place these changes in, such as the way the roads were made, the traffic on the roads.

▶ Challenge the children to carry out some of their own research to find the names of famous Roman roads around the world. Ask them to also find out the way they were made, the countries they went through, why they were made, and so on. Collect all the information the children find and make a class book about Roman roads.

▶ Ask the children to carry out similar research into famous modern roads around the world, such as the Pan-American highway. Ask them to write brief notes from their findings.

▶ Get the children to use their research to compare the way a modern road is made with Roman road-making techniques.

Farming in 1920

This photograph shows an aspect of farming around 1920. The people in the picture are using a steam thresher on a farm in Wimpole, Cambridgeshire. They are making use of what would have been considered modern technology for the time, a steam engine, to power the machine. By 1920 farms were starting to use tractor engines to power threshers, but this farm is still using steam power. The work of harvesting had always been a very labour-intensive task throughout history, even to the extent that the school holidays were timed so that children could help out. This photograph shows that several people are needed to help with the threshing process, despite the fact that they have steam power to assist them. Threshing had always been one of the hardest jobs on the farm, since the separating of the grain from the straw, and then from the chaff, was a very hard, labour-intensive task. The threshing machine would be manned by two men standing on top, one receiving the sheaves and cutting the binding, while the other fed them, head first, into the beaters inside the thresher. The grain would then be sifted from the chaff. The grain would flow into sacks attached to the back of the thresher. The straw would be ejected by large paddles, and collected by more men with pitchforks, to be made into a new rick. The straw would be used to make winter bedding for the farm animals.

Modern farming

By sharp contrast with the 'Farming in 1920' photograph, this photograph of barley being harvested on a modern farm shows how few people are now needed for this kind of task. Only the driver of the harvester is needed and the work can be completed in a much shorter time than when it was done by hand. Prior to this technology, the crops would have had to be cut and gathered by hand, before being tied up into sheaves ready for threshing. The combine harvester is able to carry out each of these separate tasks. Although expensive, most farmers today rely on this type of modern technology at harvest time. Because of its speed the modern harvester is more likely to get in the crops before they are damaged by bad weather, which was always a source of great anxiety for farmers in the past. A bad storm just before a harvest could ruin an entire year's crops. The modern combine harvester, shown here, can cut and process the grain all at the same time with no human labour involved.

Discussing the photographs

▶ Look at the photograph 'Farming in 1920' with the children. Ask them what they think is being shown.

▶ Discuss the period that the photograph is from and how long ago this was.

▶ Discuss what kind of crop the children think is being harvested, and tell them it is probably wheat.

▶ Ask the children if they can see any machinery that is being used. Discuss the use of the steam engine in industry at the time and explain how it was used to power all kinds of machinery.

▶ Note how many people are working at this one job. Explain the different kinds of jobs that are involved in threshing and talk about how different people were needed for each of these processes. Discuss the meaning of the term *labour intensive* with the children, and explain how people of all ages and backgrounds used to have to stop their normal activities in the past to help with farm work.

▶ Look with the class at the 'Modern farming' photograph, and ask the children what is being shown here.

▶ Discuss what is different between the two farming photographs.

▶ Ask the children why they think hardly any people are needed to carry out threshing on a modern farm.

▶ Discuss the work of the combine harvester, and explain how the name arose. Talk about the speed at which the combine harvester can gather in the harvest and ask the class what the advantages of this are for the modern farmer.

▶ Ask if anyone has ever ridden on a combine harvester, and get them to describe what it was like.

Activities

▶ Give the children the word cards on photocopiable page 74 and ask them to identify words that fit the dates of the two photographs, such as *century* and *ancestor*.

▶ Challenge the children to find out about the daily routine of farmers, both in the past and in the present. Suggest they create a chart or a 'clock' to show what the farmers have to do, in order to make comparison easier.

▶ Take the hot seat in the role of a late Victorian farmer or farm worker, and answer the children's questions about farming in the past.

Edinburgh in the past

This old black-and-white photograph shows Edinburgh as it was at the turn of the last century. A striking feature of the picture is the heavy pollution that seems to drift across the entire city. The sky can hardly be seen for the dense smoke that fills the air, and a lot of the rooftops of the buildings are obscured by the haze. The pollution, so evident in this picture, was caused by the smoke from domestic and industrial coal burning, and the effects of this can be clearly seen in this photograph.

The buildings are densely packed together and the only features that rise above them are the church steeples and tall factory chimneys. The castle can be seen high up in the top left-hand corner of the photograph, while most of the rest of the city appears to be filled with tall tenement blocks, all very close together and with little space between them. Inside these blocks, the small flats, known as *houses*, were very dark, as only one room would have a window. Many people often lived in one flat, making overcrowding a serious problem. Many of the large blocks would have been lodging houses, sometimes containing hundreds of lodgers, made up of men who were down on their luck.

Modern Edinburgh

This second photograph of Edinburgh in the present day is taken from almost the same position as the photograph of 'Edinburgh in the past'. It shows the castle in the distance and provides a good overview of the city. The photograph clearly has many advantages over the old picture, since it uses more advanced technology to produce a clearer image and it is also in colour. However, despite these obvious differences, it is still true to say that the city itself looks very different today compared with late Victorian times. The sky is visible and looks blue, since there appears to be no pollution from coal smoke, a result of a series of Clean Air Acts, passed in 1956, 1968 and 1993. The buildings in the foreground have all been rebuilt, and while they are still very tall, they are designed in such a way as to provide some space and light for the residents, instead of being closely packed together as in Victorian times. The city and its buildings look cleaner and brighter, and there certainly seem to be some open spaces and greenery.

Discussing the photographs

▶ Look with the class at the two photographs of Edinburgh at the same time so that they can be more easily compared. Discuss the characteristic features of each photograph.

▶ Focus on the photograph of 'Edinburgh in the past' and ask the children to point out the features they think are the most striking, such as the smoke. Can the children suggest what is creating all the smoke?

▶ Talk about what it must have been like to live in Edinburgh at this time, and consider the kinds of illnesses that people might have suffered from due to the smoke.

▶ Encourage the children to look at the detail in the photograph of 'Edinburgh in the past', and to comment on the homes that they can see. Focus their attention on how close together the buildings are, and how few green or open areas there are around them. Ask, *Where would the children play?* Explain that the tall buildings were called *tenements* and that many people lived in them.

▶ Now focus on the photograph 'Modern Edinburgh'. Discuss the reasons why this photograph looks so much better than the earlier one (it is in colour, it has been taken with a more advanced camera).

▶ Discuss whether these are all the reasons for the poor quality of the old photograph. Point out that Edinburgh is a cleaner city today by highlighting the lack of smoke in the photograph 'Modern Edinburgh'.

▶ Discuss what changes have taken place in Edinburgh in the time between the two photographs being taken, and ask for volunteers to comment on things that have changed. Can they suggest why these changes may have taken place?

▶ Ask the children what they can see that has stayed the same in the two photographs.

▶ Discuss with the children which Edinburgh they would prefer to live in and why.

Activities

▶ Provide charcoal and pastels for the children to make their own pictures of old Edinburgh in the smoke. Make a class display of these.

▶ Challenge the children to find out about the history of Edinburgh from reference books and from the Internet, and set them the task of completing a timeline of their own to show their findings. You may need to provide support in the form of an outline or template of a timeline for them to complete.

▶ Challenge very able children to research the Clean Air Acts and how they had an impact on pollution in towns and cities, such as Edinburgh. They could use the Internet or reference books to inform their research.

Covent Garden in the past

This early photograph shows Covent Garden in London at the turn of the last century. It has many of the features of a rural market, despite the fact that it is in London. The front of the buildings, for example, are obscured by traders' stalls, which are set out like a market place in a country area. Cart horses and wagons are being used to bring in the goods. The place looks busy and business-like, with people walking around engaged in the day's business.

Covent Garden Market has a very long history, dating back to Saxon times, when it is thought that stalls were there for selling produce. The existing market structure was built in 1830, and looked then very much the same as it does today. In 1872 new cast iron and glass roofs were created to cover the market halls.

Modern Covent Garden

Covent Garden in the present day has a very different appearance. In 1974, it was decided to move the market stalls and traders out of the area to Nine Elms in Vauxhall, and restoration work on the 19th-century buildings began. In 1980, Covent Garden was opened as Europe's first speciality shopping and entertainment centre. The area now has restaurants, pubs, shops, the Royal Opera House, theatres, a sports centre and many street performers. Many regard it as one of the best entertainment centres in London and it has become a popular place for tourists. Instead of the busy workman-like nature of the old Covent Garden, the new one is a place for relaxation and recreation. The buildings and cobbled areas remain as they were in Victorian times, however, many of the stalls have been replaced by open-air cafés and comfortable seating.

Discussing the photographs

▶ Display the two photographs of Covent Garden side by side and ask the children to identify which is the old scene and which the new. Ask them to give reasons for their decision.

▶ Challenge the children to point out the characteristic architectural features that suggest the 'Covent Garden in the past' photograph is Victorian, such as the iron structure and glass roofs.

▶ Look at the 'Modern Covent Garden' photograph and discuss how this is a mixture of old and modern styles. Discuss why this is.

▶ Ask the children to identify the features in the modern photograph that are Victorian and those that are modern.

▶ Tell the children how long ago Covent Garden began as a market, and how today it is still a market but is also a major tourist attraction in London with leisure facilities as well as shops in its complex of buildings.

▶ Ask if anyone has ever been to Covent Garden and ask them to describe their memories of what they saw there.

Activities
▶ Help the children to locate Covent Garden on a map of London.
▶ If possible, organise a visit to Covent Garden, where the children can make firsthand observations of the points they have previously discussed about the architecture and the nature of modern Covent Garden.
▶ Challenge the children to find out in greater detail about the activities they could do or things they could buy at new Covent Garden, by asking adults or by using the Internet.

Canal boats in the past

This photograph shows working canal boats at the turn of the last century. The narrowboats, or barges, appear to be coming along the canal in a procession. Each one is connected to a horse by a towrope, which is just visible. Large shire horses were used to tow the boats along, and each one needed a person to lead them and make sure they continued to pull their boat along. It is because of this method of moving the boats along that there are towpaths alongside canals today. Controlling the horses must have been a fairly skilled job, to ensure that no problems or accidents occurred. The boats had to be 'walked' through tunnels, as most didn't have towpaths inside them. This involved people lying on top of the narrowboat and 'walking' their feet along the roof of the tunnel in order to move the barge through it. In earlier times and well into the Victorian period, these narrowboats were used to ship heavy goods, particularly coal, around the country, since this was easier, faster and cheaper than moving them by road.

Modern canal boats

These same narrowboats can still be seen on the canalways today. In fact, it is now a popular way to spend recreational time. The interiors of the barges used for leisure purposes are converted from facilities for carrying large quantities of cargo, such as coal, into simple living quarters. These house a small galley kitchen, an eating area, space for bunks to sleep in and a small bathroom. People hire them out for the day or for a holiday of a week or more, so that they can enjoy boating through the canals. There are lots of features along the canalside, such as pubs, hotels and inns. These were frequently used by people on the working barges in the past. Although the towpaths still run alongside the canals, the boats now tend to be powered by diesel engines. Some boats are still used as working boats today, however, to transport goods around the country, and some people choose to live on canal boats.

Discussing the photographs
▶ Compare the two photographs with the children and discuss what they show.
▶ Ask the children to suggest when each of the photographs were taken.
▶ Ask for volunteers to point out what is the same about the boats and what has changed.
▶ Discuss how the boats have the same design and structure in both photographs, but how they have been adapted over time. Can anyone suggest why this is? Explain that it is because their use has changed from being used to carry cargo around the country to leisure boats. Explain how the old holds have been converted into living quarters on the modern boats.
▶ Talk about the way the boats moved in the past compared with the present day. Discuss the modern use of diesel-powered engines.
▶ Discuss the environmental considerations of the way the two boats were powered. Can the children suggest which method is better for the environment? What are the advantages and disadvantages of both methods?
▶ Ask the children if they have seen large horses like those used in the photograph 'Canal boats in the past'. Discuss what they are called and some of the work they used to do (pulling heavy carts on farms).
▶ Ask the children how they think the canal boats in the past got through the tunnels. Tell them how the boats were 'walked' though the tunnels.
▶ Ask if anyone has ever been to a canal and walked along a towpath, or been on a canal boat. Discuss the peace and quiet of the way of life.
▶ Point out to the children the great dangers associated with canals, because of their unknown depth and the steep sides. Discuss how today they are quite polluted and diseases can be caught from the water. Discuss also how locks are even more dangerous because of the depth of water flowing through them, and the speed at which the water gushes into them.

Activities

▶ Help the children to locate some of the major canals on a map of Britain, such as the Bridgewater Canal, Grand Union Canal, the Manchester Ship Canal, Trent and Mersey Canal.

▶ Challenge the children to research the history of the canalways in Britain and to find out how old some of the canals are and some of the people involved in their construction, such as James Brindley and Thomas Telford.

▶ Revise some of the key vocabulary related to the pictures, such as *towpath*, *towrope*, *narrow boat*.

▶ If possible, organise a visit to a local canal and explain to them how locks work.

Coventry in 1905

This is a photograph of the Foleshill Road in Coventry in 1905. Like other photographs of streets at this time, the photograph shows what seems to us today to be a rather empty scene. There is no traffic in the road at all, and clearly it is not usual to find traffic there, since there is a man walking in the middle of the road. The tram lines suggest that there is a tram service, however. People seem to travel mainly on foot and some use bicycles – one can be seen just in the bottom left-hand corner of the picture, propped against a shop window. The shops and their clients are carefully shaded by blinds drawn down to cover the windows and the goods in them. This would have been important in days before fridges and refrigerated display units were available. Tall lampposts and telegraph poles are the only street furniture. The large building with the sign at the top of it is the General Wolf, which was a prominent inn at the time.

Modern Coventry (1)

This photograph shows the same section of the Foleshill Road as in the photograph 'Coventry in 1905'. It has been taken in the early evening when the shops have closed for the day. The street is the same in many ways as the old photograph – it is wide and spacious, and the buildings are easily recognisable when comparing them. The shop fronts are obviously modern with metal pull-down covers to protect them overnight. However, closer inspection also shows how some of the names on the shop fronts reflect a wide variety of goods on offer. There is a bank, a typical sight on most high streets, and a shop called the 'Indian meat shop'. In modern times, most city centres, and areas around them, reflect the multicultural makeup of society within the area. The shops, therefore, need to cater for the requirements of people with many divergent backgrounds. In many towns and cities today it is easy to find shops selling a range of food and ingredients, ranging from Indian, Chinese, Italian, Thai, Greek and Spanish. Many of these foods have become a regular part of the British diet. Other kinds of shops also reflect the multicultural nature of society today, from banks from different parts of the world to fashion shops.

Modern Coventry (2)

This photograph shows another part of the Foleshill Road, and clearly shows the multicultural makeup of towns and cities in Britain today. A large Asian supermarket takes up a whole row of buildings that would probably have been several small shops in the past. Supermarkets like this one are popular with all sections of the community, since Asian food is widely enjoyed and many people who are not Asian are beginning to develop the skills to cook Asian food at home. Like the very early shops in the 'Coventry in 1905' photograph, this shop has blinds drawn down to protect the fruit and vegetables on sale outside from the heat of the sun. The road outside appears busy, and like the photograph 'Modern Coventry (1)' it shows the place that traffic has taken up in modern towns and cities. The road here is dominated by the traffic lights and there are barriers to prevent accidents at the crossing place.

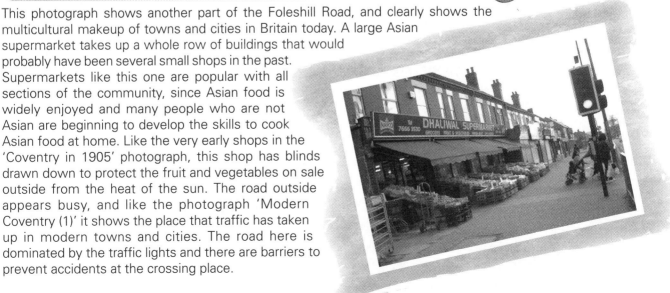

Discussing the photographs

▶ Look at all three photographs together with the class, and discuss when they were taken. Point out that one was taken 100 years ago, while the other two are modern.

▶ Apart from the superficial differences between the photographs – that the modern ones are in colour and the old one in black and white – ask the children what differences they can make out between the two periods of photographs.

▶ Discuss what changes have taken place in 100 years and ask for volunteers to comment on the things that have changed.

▶ Ask the children what they can see that has stayed the same.

▶ Talk about the new kinds of shops that have appeared since 1905 that can be seen in the modern photographs. Ask the children why they think there are now new and different shops.

▶ Discuss why people have moved to Britain from other parts of the world since 1905. Talk about the many places that people have moved from, and relate this to the shops shown in the 'Modern Coventry (1) and (2)' photographs.

▶ Discuss the notion of *multicultural* with the children, explaining what it means. Also discuss the meaning of *immigration* with the children in relation to this.

Activities

▶ Ask the children to make a 'similarities and differences' chart to list the changes they can see between the two photographs.

▶ If possible, make a class visit to a nearby town centre, where changes of the kind shown in these three photographs can be seen. Get the children to make notes and sketches, and to take photographs of places that show they live in a multicultural society.

▶ Carry out a class debate about issues that arise from changes in society. For example, debate the advantages of having a mixture of cultures and religions within a community. Care will be needed to avoid any potentially adverse or harmful comment being made about any refugees you have in your class or those from different cultural backgrounds.

▶ Invite a speaker in who can provide an oral history account of the multicultural changes in an area. Let the children use the 'Interviewing frame' (photocopiable page 80) in advance of this to formulate the sort of questions they want to ask.

NOTES ON THE PHOTOCOPIABLE PAGES

Word and sentence cards
PAGES 73–6

A number of specific types of vocabulary related to the local history theme have been introduced on the word and sentence cards:

▶ words associated with historical sources, such as *census* and *trade directory*
▶ words related to historical research, such as *century* and *generation*
▶ words associated with buildings, such as *detached*, *factory*, *arch*.

Encourage the children to make a note of other appropriate words to add to those provided, to build up a word bank for their work on local history.

Activities

▶ Make a local history display using the resources that have been used and ask the children to label these with the word and sentence cards.

▶ Encourage the children to use the word cards in extended writing tasks to record what they have learned.

▶ The children can use the sentence cards as examples of ways of writing sentences to summarise what they have learned. Ask them to create sentences of their own which include words from the word cards to summarise new learning about local history and changes in their locality.

Extract from the Domesday Book
PAGE 77

This extract on Warwick from the Domesday Book, compiled in 1086, outlines the properties in the area and also the amount of tax due from them (or their 'dues'). The King and his barons were the most important landowners, with large numbers of houses. It is interesting to note that some houses had to be demolished in order to start the building of the castle. Another interesting feature is the different names of the property and landowners. While some have French names, denoting their Norman origins, such as Geoffrey of La Guerche or William Bonvallet, others have Saxon or Viking names, such as Harold and Thorkell. This tells us that the Norman invasion does not appear to have resulted in the previous landlords losing all their property rights.

The list of 'dues' shows how the area had been known as the Sheriffdom of Warwick. It had already been paying taxes to its previous landlords, thus suggesting that there was probably little real change in the lives of ordinary people with the arrival of the Normans – they simply had new masters to pay their taxes to. Dogs, horses and hawks were taxed and, interestingly, honey features as a highly significant source of revenue. This was because at that time there was no sugar in Europe, since it had not yet been discovered, and so honey was a valued commodity.

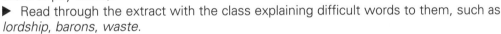

Discussing the document

▶ Look at the title of the document and ask the children if they have ever heard of the Domesday book before.

▶ Discuss what the Domesday Book was (a survey of the houses in the country, carried out on the orders of William the Conqueror after he had invaded England).

▶ Discuss why the book was made (so that the king could find out how many people there were in his new land and then order them to pay taxes).

▶ Read through the extract with the class explaining difficult words to them, such as *lordship*, *barons*, *waste*.

▶ Talk about what the first part of the extract is describing (the number of houses owned by different people).

▶ Can the children work out who the largest property owners were.

▶ Explain what the last two paragraphs of the extract outline and look at the sort of things that had to have taxes paid on them.

▶ Talk about why hawks should have been singled out for taxation (they were used extensively for hunting).

▶ Explain what packhorses were and consider why taxes were paid on these (a person used them to make money by transporting goods on them).

▶ Discuss and explain to the children why honey is mentioned so often.

Activities

▶ Challenge the children to find out the origin of the word *Domesday* (from *domus*, Latin for *house* or *home*). Ask them to find other words with the same origin, such as *domestic*, *domicile*.

▶ Discuss what some of the very ancient words in the extract mean, such as *burgess* (member of the governing body of a town). Ask the children to look these up and write their own definitions of them.

▶ Organise the children into groups to conduct research into William the Conqueror, the Domesday Book, barons, boroughs, manors and so on, and to make notes so that they can tell the class about their findings at the end of the allocated time.

▶ Take on the role of William the Conqueror and answer questions from the children about why you have ordered the Domesday Book to be made. Let the children use the 'Interviewing frame' (photocopiable page 80) to record notes before and during the interview.

Photograph © Ingram Publishing

Census form

PAGE 78

This simplified blank 'census form' is intended for children to use themselves. A copy can be completed by each child about their own household (be sensitive to any children who might not want to share details about their home). Possibly the best way to make use of the form is to give it to the children to complete at home. Their families and carers can then also be involved in its completion and also in the topic work that is taking place.

If the children can compare their own house in the past and the present, this will be a very interesting and motivating activity for them.

Research checklist
PAGE 79

The checklist can be used by children when studying maps of their area from a different time in the past and in the present. It could be used either with map work related to your own locality, or with the maps provided on the CD. The checklist may also be useful for the children to use when out on a local history or local studies walk. They will need to have studied maps and information about their locality before going on the walk, of course, in order to be able to identify changes that have taken place. Perhaps the easiest things for children to find will be places that have changed their use, such as churches or chapels, for example, which may have been converted into houses or offices.

Interviewing frame
PAGE 80

The interviewing frame is a simple writing frame that is intended to help children collect the sort of information that they need when interviewing people. If information is to be built up over a period of time, then they will realise the need to record the date and time of their interviews. They will also understand the need to record the names of those involved, especially if a class book is to be made, or if they intend to write about their findings at a later date. It teaches them the need to be methodical, an important aspect of historical research. The frame also encourages them to make a note of the questions they intend to ask prior to the interview.

Historical sources word cards

census

trade directory

street directory

oral history

documents

Census returns are useful sources for finding out about people who lived in a locality at different times.

Historical research word cards

decade

century

generation

ancestor

A person from a different generation can talk about life in an earlier decade, or even from an earlier century.

Buildings word cards (1)

factory

mill

storey

detached

semi-detached

architecture

Buildings word cards (2)

sash window

steeple

gable

arch

Sash windows and tall buildings with several storeys are characteristic features of Victorian architecture.

Extract from the Domesday Book

In the Borough of Warwick:
the King has 113 houses in his lordship and the King's barons have 112, from all of which the King has his tax.

The Bishop of Worcester has 9 dwellings; the Bishop of Chester 7; the Abbot of Coventry 36; and 4 are waste, because of the castle site.
The Bishop of Coutances has 1 house; the Count of Meulan 12 dwellings. Earl Aubrey had 4, which belong to the land which he held; Hugh of Grandmesnil 4, and the monks of Pillerton have 1 from him. Henry of Ferrers has 2, Harold 2, Robert of Stafford 6, Roger of Ivry 2, Richard Hunter 1, Ralph of Limesy 9, the Abbot of Malmesbury 1, William Bonvallet 1, William son of Corbucion 2, Geoffrey de Mandeville 1, Geoffrey of La Guerche 1, Gilbert of Ghent 2, Gilbert [of] Bouille 1, Nicholas the Gunner 1, Stephen the Steersman 1, Thorkell 4, Harold 2, Osbern son of Richard 1, Christina 1, the nun Leofeva 2.

These dwellings belong to the lands which these barons hold outside the Borough and are there assessed.

Besides the said dwellings, there are 19 burgesses in this Borough who have 19 dwellings, with full jurisdiction and all customary dues, and had them thus before 1066.

Before 1066 the Sheriffdom of Warwick, with the Borough and with the royal manors, paid £65 and 36 sesters of honey, or £24 8s for all that belonged to the honey. Now the revenue of the royal manors and the pleas of the County between them pay £145 a year by weight, £23 for dog-custom, 20s for a packhorse, £10 for a hawk and 100s for gifts to the Queen.

Besides this, it pays 24 sesters of honey, with the larger measure, and from the Borough 6 sesters of honey, that is, a sester at 15 pence. Of these, the Count of Meulan has 6 sesters and 5s.

Census form

Year	County	Town or village or hamlet										

Census

Road, street and number or name of house	Name of each person who lives at the house	Relation to head of the family	Age last birthday	Profession or occupation	Place of birth							

Research checklist

▷ When using sources to find out about changes in an area, use the following checklist to guide your research. You may want to make this checklist bigger by adding other things relevant to your area.

Things I can find that have been added to the area:	Things I can see that have stayed the same:
New streets made ☐	Streets ☐
New footpaths ☐	Roads ☐
New churches ☐	Rivers and streams ☐
New factories ☐	Factories, mills, mines ☐
Railway lines ☐	Churches, cathedrals ☐
	Open fields and spaces ☐

Things I can see that have been removed:	Things I can see that have remained in the same place, but have changed their name and their use:
Inns ☐	Churches ☐
Churches ☐	Factories, mills ☐
Factories ☐	Fields ☐
Fields ☐	

Interviewing frame

Topic or subject of interview	Date and time

Interviewee	Interviewer

Question	Response